How to Analyze People Mastery

The Ultimate Collection To Think And Analyze People Like Sherlock Holmes Using Rapid Deduction Techniques, Advanced Speed Reading Strategies And Proven Body Language Methods

Patrick Lightman

How to Analyze People Mastery:
The Ultimate Collection To Think And Analyze People Like
Sherlock Holmes Using Proven Body Language Methods,
Advanced Speed Reading Strategies And Rapid Deduction
Techniques
Copyright © 2019 by Patrick Lightman

How To Analyze People 1:
A Psychologist's Guide to Human Behavior, Body Language, Personality Types and Reading People

Introduction 7

Chapter 1: Human Psychology Basics Decoded ... 15

Chapter 2: Body Language and Voice Basics
Revealed 31

Chapter 3: Reading People Through Personality
Types 49

Chapter 4: Effectively Analyzing People Through
Their Words 79

Chapter 5: Personality and Birth Order 92

Conclusion 102

How To Analyze People 2:

Rapid Deduction Techniques To Think And Analyze People Like Sherlock Holmes

Introduction 105

Chapter 1: Analyzing People Through Their Handwriting 112

Chapter 2: Tips For Uncovering Insights About Other People's Values 126

Chapter 3: Reading People Through Their Immediate Environment 138

Chapter 4: Judging a Book by Its Cover 149

Chapter 5: Speed Reading People Through Their Photographs 159

Chapter 6: Spotting Deception Through Non-Verbal Clues 172

Chapter 7: The Attraction Body Language 190

Conclusion... 198

How to Analyze People 1

A Psychologist's Guide to Human Behavior, Body Language, Personality Types and Reading People

Patrick Lightman

Introduction

If I were to ask you, "What is the single most important skill that will give in an edge over others in a personal, professional and social set-up?", what would your answer be? Think about it carefully. We are social creatures and our ability to succeed in life pretty much depends on our ability to understand people. Throughout our lives, a majority of our time is spend in interaction with people (unless you live in a cardboard box or rabbit hole) and developing new associations. If you were to ask me for the single biggest vital survival and success skill in today's world, it would undoubtedly be the art of analyzing people.

How will you figure out if a prospective employee is a perfect fit for your organizational values and goals? How will you determine if the attractive new lady/man you fancy will be a positive and inspiring long-term mate? How will you identify if a potential client is worth doing business with?

How will you cut winsome deals with the right business partners and associates?

How will you forge rewarding business connections at networking events? The master key to all of the above lies in your ability to analyze people, identify their personality, recognize how they think and feel, and above all, communicate in a relevant or appropriate manner based on their personality or behavior.

What is it that primarily drives and motivates people? What is the main personality type? What does their body language reveal about their subconscious thoughts? When you learn to analyze people and identify their fundamental personality type and their thought patterns, you can communicate with them in a more effective and meaningful manner.

When you have the ability to analyze people's behavior and personality, you have an edge when it comes to adapting your own words and actions to develop a winsome rapport with the other person, thus forming more productive and fulfilling interpersonal relationships or professional associations. Well, analyzing people isn't just vital for FBI sleuths but also for regular, everyday people to form more beneficial connections.

Learning to analyze people is one of the most effective and sharpest skills one can develop in today's fast-paced world where there is no escaping the importance of forming new connections and constantly interacting with people in a frenzied pace. The power to tune in to obvious and subtle clues people give out all the time will equip you with the super power to deliver a message more persuasively or convincingly to a person. When you understand how people think and feel, you'll deliver a message in a manner that is suitable for their thought patterns and actions, thus minimizing the chances of misunderstanding.

You will wield greater control over a conversation or enhance your negotiation skills. People who possess the ability to analyze and read others make for more empathetic friends, partners, employer and leaders. You'll be a razor-sharp businessman and negotiator. As a salesperson or business development person, you'll know exactly what your customer or client wants, which will help boost your sales figures. The scope for conflict-ridden situations will reduce when you understand other people's limitations and structure your communication to suit them.

In short, the skill of reading or analyzing people will determine the quality of relationships you enjoy in life. When you master the tips, techniques and strategies for reading people, you know what to look for while attempting to understand them. What are the unspoken things that are given away by their body language? What does their choice of words reveal about people's personality and attitudes? What is their essential character or personality type? How can you tell if someone is telling the truth or resorting to deception? How can you tell if someone is just being themselves or pretending to be something they clearly aren't?

Monthly glossies have done a lot of disservice to the art of analyzing people by reducing it to pop quizzes such as "What your favorite food says about you" or "What does your favorite lipstick shade reveal about your persona?" It isn't as trivial as marketers or glossy editors have us believe. Analyzing people is about delving into people's minds and understanding their words, thoughts, actions and behavior through psychology-driven principles. It is a comprehensive and deep study that has several factors involved.

Much as you'd like to believe, your favorite fragrance doesn't say much about your personality. It can be highly entertaining and addictive but isn't even remotely accurate. To be a star people analyzer, you need plenty of practice, and the ability to decode personalities.

Though this is a highly intensive field of study involving dynamics of psychology, human behavior, social skills and more, in this book I am packing the most concise, practical and actionable tips that will get you started with reading people. These techniques can be applied just about anywhere, from your workplace to personal relationships to social life. The sky is the limit when you develop the ability to understand people and influence them using this understanding.

According to research, the ability to analyze people can help us predict the outcome of a negotiation correctly in around 80 percent of all instances. Doesn't that give you an edge when it comes to steering a negotiation in the right direction?

However, let's get started with some valuable fundamental people analyzing rules that will help you set you on the path for being an ace people reader.

Humans are invariably wired throughout primitive times to interact with each other via subconscious signals. Sometimes, people may appear to be happy and content on the face of it, but deep inside their subconscious mind they may harbor feelings of resentment, frustration and disappointment. When you learn to watch out for these clues, you can reach out to people more effectively.

What is a person's primary instinct or gut feeling? What we refer to as our gut feeling or instinct is nothing but our ability to latch on to specific clues that a person transmits at a subconscious level.

When a person smiles, our smile muscles are reflexively triggered at a more subconscious level. Therefore when someone smiles at us, we smile instinctively in return. Human brains are created to capture clues that are not apparent to the conscious mind. For instance, think about the time when a person was behaving in a pleasant and positive manner, yet you experienced a strong sense of discomfort while dealing with them. This is because our minds are wired to latch on to subconscious signals.

It may be something about the person's body language, including high blood pressure, faster heart beat, increased palpitations, sweating and more that our mind catches at a more subconscious level that gives us the feeling that something isn't quite right. This explains why sometimes you just don't like some people even when you don't know them well enough to identify their personality.

Chapter One: Human Psychology Basics Decoded

If you track the human evolutionary pattern, you will understand that our brains are wired to conduct accurate readings about our thoughts, actions and behavior. In the absence of language in primitive ages, how did human beings communicate with each other? They communicated through the medium of tone, voice, expression, gestures, postures, signs and other non-verbal mediums. This implies that the skill of reading people already exists within us. It simply needs to be fine-tuned at a conscious level to help us form more productive and fulfilling relationships.

Everyone from trial attorneys to detectives to salespersons to employers can use people analyzing skills to their advantage. Did you know that high-end car salespersons are trained to peep inside their prospective customer's cars to understand their customers better and strike a rapport with them through small talk? If a salesperson sees a golf kit in the back seat of the car, they'll start a conversation about how they enjoy playing golf over the weekends or about a recent golf championship.

Then trial attorneys will attempt to decode where the jury is swinging simply by observing non-verbal clues offered by the jurors while witnesses, officials or the defendant is being cross examined in the stands. They will also brief their clients about maintaining a body language that generally gives out a positive overall impression about him or her to jurors. This can mean eliminating all non-verbal clues that reveal deception or trickery.

Also, when you learn to analyze people, you view them in a more objective and non-judgmental manner. You will also learn to pick up on clues that reveal deception or untruthful behavior. Let us take an example where people try to manipulate you or get what they want using false flattery.

When you master the art of reading people, you will be able to determine if people truly feel those compliments from within or they are simply resorting to fake flattery to get what they want. This helps you protect yourself against other people's vested interests.

Here are some amazing advantages of being a people analyzer:

- You are able to enjoy more fulfilling and rewarding interpersonal relationships, thus reducing the pain of unsuitable relationships. You don't want to kiss a thousand frogs to find that one prince/princess, do you?

- It saves you the time, energy and effort of eliminating toxic people and dealing with only those who match your own objectives, values and expectations. People who sap your energy can be shown the door.

- The ability to analyze people can save you tons of money and hours by hiring employees that are a right fit for your organization.

- As a partner or employer, you can tell when people are being deceitful in a relationship or during an interview. You can select a long-term partner who matches not just your own personality but also your values, personality, behavioral traits and more. It will help you weed out dates whose objectives and expectations do not match your own.

- Analyzing people makes you a more power-packed leader. You'll understand your team's goals, motivations, triggers and much more, which can be effectively leveraged for optimizing their performance. This may lead to greater productivity and overall job satisfaction. Learning to read people can be your highway to professional success.

- It is a vital skill when it comes to carrying out negotiations and sales deals. When you figure out how a person prospective client, business associate or customer is thinking, it is simpler to divert the negotiation to your advantage. For instance, if the other party's body language and other non-verbal clues communicate that they are happy with the negotiation terms, yet they ask for a better deal, you know you have to stick your ground because they are simply trying their luck now. Once you realize they are already sold, you won't make any further concessions.

- Reading people helps you fine tune your own verbal and non-verbal communication for creating a dazzling first impression. It helps you package yourself exactly as you want to create more beneficial connections and relationships. You can position yourself as a genuine, credible, friendly and authoritative individual based on the situation by sending the right verbal and non-verbal clues.

- Your empathy factor increases, and you are able to understand people or reach out to them in troubled times more effectively to form more productive interpersonal relationships.

- You increase your chances of performing well at job interviews by sending the right verbal and non-verbal signals to recruiters. You know how to create the right impression by communicating the values, characteristics and ideals that are appropriate for a specific organization or role.

- Tuning in to other people's body language and verbal communication skills makes you an effective speaker. When you gather clues for your audience's body language, you know exactly what they are thinking or feeling about what you're saying. Are they bored, inspired or suspicious about what you are saying? Do they disagree with what you are saying? This will help you quickly change and adapt your speech to evoke a more favorable response. You will be able to say the right things to strike a chord with your audience and persuade them. As a speaker, you'll discover a common ground for connecting with your audience for better results.

- Your chances of electing leaders, politicians and influencers with the right vision will increase when you learn to understand people's motives through their body language, personality, voice and words.

Learn to identify traits that make for a powerful and positive influencer such as integrity, authority, generosity, empathy and more. You will be able to recognize people who truly care about others from those who display vested interests for grabbing power.

People are much like onions. They have multiple personality layers that have to be peeled off to glimpse into their real personality characteristics. Some layers of your personality are apparent, while others are inconspicuous. Sometimes, even we are unable to figure out who we really are because we seem like such a bundle of contradictions to ourselves.

A people analyzer or reader can quickly decipher an individual's personality through several attributes, including what he or she does in their spare time. For example, if you inquire what a person does in their spare time and they reveal they participate in community drives, volunteering activities or contribute to church initiatives, you know they are philanthropic, magnanimous or community conscious. Similarly, if a person says they love partying endlessly or watching television in their free time, they may be low on ambition or seek quick gratification. The point is, even something as seemingly trivial as what a person does in his or her spare time can reveal his or her personality.

Theories of Human Behavior

Classical Conditioning

Classical Conditioning is a popular psychological theory through which people learn by pairing behavior as stimuli and response to the stimuli. This principle is used for training animals too. Don't you reward your dog with a treat each time it fetches the ball? In the pet's mind, fetching is closely associated with treats or rewards, so it invariably learns that it has to fetch the ball if wants to be rewarded with a treat.

All through our life as human beings, classical conditioning helps shape our behavior. As babies, we come to associate crying with being fed and kept clean. Students learn that studying consistently and dedicatedly gets you good grades. Thus, classical conditioning influences our behavior and acts throughout our lives. We learn to respond to a specific stimuli in a particular manner. It is one of the main factors when it comes to determining an individual's behavior.

Human Behavior and Physiology

According to research, people have peculiar physical reactions to certain stimuli that are valuable when it comes to analyzing them. These principles are usually used in the area of criminal psychology to understand how criminals think and what drives them to commit crimes. With the help of biometric technology investigators attempt to identify if the suspect's thoughts are in sync with their actions.

This combination of psychological and physiological techniques is powerful for analyzing the underlying motives of human behavior. The human body undergoes specific physiological reactions when a person is misleading or lying. The reaction can be standalone clues or a combination of dilated pupils, increase in heart rate, greater palpitations, sweating and twitching toes. Physiology or non-verbal clues can help you analyze a person more accurately, though much like other people analyzing theories, it can never be fool proof.

Experiences and Human Behavior

While certain psychologists are of the opinion that our behavior is directly determined by genetics or heredity, others believe that it is a summation of all our experiences since birth. They are of the opinion that our immediate environment or the experiences we undergo in our immediate environment mold our behavior. For example, if a person experiences constant marginalization or prejudice on account of their class or race, they may grow up to despise wealth or seemingly superior races. They may empathize with the oppressed.

Similarly, if a person is constantly bullied, abused or victimized as a child, he or she may grow up to be a bully themselves. Much of their outlook, values, personality and attitude will be shaped by these early childhood experiences or violence and abuse.

Many psychologists believe that a person is almost always drawn to things they inherently believe they lack to make up for it. For instance, people who are not sure of themselves or don't have a high self-confidence or self-esteem may constantly seek approval from others. They may look for approval and validation all the time.

Have you ever observed people who keenly attempt read their personality through zodiac signs or astrology? Isn't this a sign of possessing low self-awareness or understanding? People often gravitate towards things they believe they haven't got much of. For example, someone who hasn't been given sufficient attention by their parents during early childhood or teen years may grow up to be a person who thrives on drama and attention-seeking tactics. They may become more dramatic and showy.

There are plenty of clues everywhere. As a people analyzer, you just need to keep an eye out for these subtle clues.

Subconscious Mind and Human Behavior

Our mind is divided into three layers – the conscious mind, subconscious mind and unconscious mind. While the conscious mind or state of consciousness is awareness of thoughts, actions, learnings and experiences, the subconscious and unconscious mind are realms of the mind that hold things we may not be aware of. Through the conscious mind, we have awareness of things we perceive and feel. We can process feelings, thoughts, concepts and ideas that are gathered from our immediate environment.

However, when it comes to the subconscious and unconscious mind, we have little or no awareness of the thoughts, ideas, concepts and information stored in it. Our conscious mind is only the tip of an iceberg. There are multiple hidden layers, which influence our personality and behavior that we are not aware of.

If you want to be a power-packed people analyzer, begin with yourself. Identify how much you know about yourself or how well you understand your own personality or behavior patterns. Attempt to understand what drives you into behaving in a specific manner. What are your underlying beliefs, fears, motivators, values and more?

Once you've uncovered your own personality and behavioral characteristics, attempt to understand close friends and family members. Lastly, move to strangers who you spot while waiting at a doctor's clinic or at the supermarket/airport or someone you've only just met at a party. Keep practicing to sharpen your people analyzing skills until you are able to read people quickly and effectively, like a pro!

Emotions and Human Behavior

Emotions are brief short conscious experiences that we experience as part of our mental activity. These feelings are not based in rational or logical thoughts. For example, even in the face of compelling proof that our friend is betraying us behind our back, we don't break ties with him or her and prefer to trust them.

As humans, we are prone to acting on impulses rather than logic, reasoning and evidence. People's behaviors are fundamentally shaped by emotions. Thus, understanding people's emotions gives us the power to comprehend and predict their actions, personality and behavioral patterns.

Chapter Two: Body Language and Voice Basics Revealed

Do you know that people communicate much more through what they leave unspoken than what they actually say? Body language accounts for around 55 percent of the entire message during the process of communication. In a study conducted by Dr. Albert Mehrabian, it was revealed that only 7 percent of our message is communicated through words, while 38 percent and 55 percent is conveyed through non-verbal elements such as vocal factors and body language, respectively.

Generally, what people say is well-thought and constructed within their conscious mind. This makes it easier to manipulate or fake words for creating a desired impression. Our body language, on the other hand, is guided by more involuntary movements of the subconscious mind. It is near impossible to fake subconsciously driven actions that we aren't even aware of. When you train yourself to look for non-verbal clues, you understand an individual's thoughts, feelings, actions and more at a deeper, subconscious level. Try controlling the thoughts held within your subconscious mind and you'll know what I am saying.

People are perpetually sending subconscious signals and clues while interacting with us, a majority of which we miss because we are conditioned to focus on their words. Since primitive times, human communicated through the power of gestures, symbols, expressions and more in the absence of a coherent language. You have the power to influence and persuade people through the use of body language on a deeply subconscious level since it's so instinctive and reflex driven.

Here are some of the most powerful body language decoding secrets that will help you unlock hidden clues held in the subconscious mind, and read people more effectively.

Establish a Behavior Baseline

Create a baseline for understanding a person's behavior if you want to read him or her more effectively. This is especially true when you are meeting people for the first time, and want to guard against forming inaccurate conclusions about people's behavior. Establishing a baseline guards you against misreading people by making sweeping judgments about their personality, feelings and behavior.

Establishing a baseline is nothing but determining the baseline personality of individual based on which you can read the person more effectively rather than making generic readings based on body language. For instance, if a person is more active, fast-thinking and impatient by nature, they will want to get a lot of things done quickly.

They may fidget with their hands or objects, tap their feet or appear restless. If you don't establish a baseline for their behavior, you may mistake their mental energy for nervousness or disinterest, since the clues are almost similar. You would mistakenly believe the person is anxious when he/she is hyperactive.

Observe and tune in to an individual completely to understand their baseline. This helps you examine both verbal and non-verbal clues in a context. How does a person generally react in the given situation? What is their fundamental personality? How do they communicate with other people? What type of words do they generally use? Are they essentially confident or unsure by nature?

When you know how they normally behave, you'll be able to catch a mismatch in their baseline and unusual behavior, which will make the reading even more effective.

Look For a Cluster of Clues

One of the biggest mistakes people make while analyzing others through non-verbal clues is looking for isolated or standalone clues instead of a bunch of clues. Your chances of reading a person accurately increases when you look at several clues that point to a single direction rather than making sweeping conclusions based on isolated clues. For instance, let us say you've read in a book about body language that people who resort to deception or aren't speaking the truth don't look a person directly in the eye.

However, it can also be a sign of being low on confidence or possessing low self-esteem. Similarly, a person may not be looking at your while speaking because he/she is directly facing discomfort causing sunlight. You ignore all other signs that point to the fact that the person is speaking the truth or is confident (a firm handshake, relaxed posture etc.) and only choose to look at the single clue that he/she isn't maintaining eye contact to inaccurately conclude that the person is lying. Look for at least 3-4 clues to arrive at a conclusion. Don't make sporadic conclusions about how a person is thinking or feeling based on single clues.

For all you know a person may be moving in another direction, not because they aren't interested in what you are speaking about or looking to escape, but because their seat is uncomfortable.

If you think the person is disinterested, look for other clues such as their expressions, gestures, eyes and more to make more accurate conclusions. Include a wider number of non verbal clues to make the analysis more accurate.

Look at the Context, Setting and Culture

Some body language clues are universal – think smile or eye contact. These signals more or less mean the same across cultures. However some non-verbal communication signals may have different connotations across diverse cultures.

For example, being gregarious and expressive is seen as common in Italian culture. People speak loudly, gesticulate with their hands in an animated manner, and are generally more expressive.

However, someone from England may decipher this behavior as massively exaggerated or a sign of nervousness. Enthusiasm, delight and excitement are expressed in a more subtle manner in England. For the Italian, this retrained behavior may signify disinterest. While the thumbs-up is a gesture of good luck in the west, in certain Middle Eastern cultures it is viewed as rude. If you are doing business with people from across the world, understanding cultural differences before reading people is vital.

Similarly, consider a setting before making sweeping conclusions through non-verbal signs such as body language. For example, a person may display drastically different behavior when he's at work among co-workers, at the bar and during a job interview. The setting and atmosphere of a job interview may make an otherwise confident person nervous.

Head and Face

People are most likely experiencing a sense of discomfort when they raise or arch their eyebrows. The facial muscles also begin twitching when they are hiding something or lying. These are micro expressions that are hard to manipulate since they happen in split seconds and are subconscious involuntary actions.

Maintaining eye contact can be a sign of both honesty and intimidation/aggression. On the other hand, constantly shifting your gaze can be a non-verbal clue of deceit.

The adage that one's eyes are a window into their soul is true. People who don't look into your eyes while speaking may not be very trustworthy. Similarly, a shifting gaze can indicate nervousness.

The human eye movements are closely linked with brain regions that perform specific functions. Hence, when we think (depending on what or how we are thinking), our eyes move in a clear direction. For example, when a person is asked for details that he/she is retrieving from memory, their eyes will move in the upper left direction. Similarly, when someone is constructing information (or making up stories) instead of recalling it from memory, their eyes will shift to the upper right direction. The exact opposite is true for left-handed folks. When people try to recall information from memory, their eyes shift to the upper left, whereas when they try to create facts, the eyes move towards the upper left corner. A person who is making fictitious sounds or talking about a conversation that didn't happen, their eyes will move to the lateral left.

When there's an inner dilemma or conflict, a person's eyes will dart towards their left collarbone. This is an indication of an inner dialogue when a person is stuck between two choices. Increased eye movement from one side to another can signal deception. Again, look for a cluster of clues rather than simply analyzing people based on their eye movements.

Expanded pupils or increased blinking is a huge sign of attraction, desire and lust. A person may also display these clues when they are interested in what you are saying. If a person sizes you up by looking at you in an upward and downward direction, they are most likely considering your potential as a sexual mate or rival. Similarly, looking at a person from head to toe can also be a sign of intimidation or dominance.

When you are observing a person's face, learn to watch out for micro expressions that are a direct involuntary response based on feelings and thoughts. These reactions are so instinctive and happen in microseconds that they are impossible to fake. For example, when a person is lying, their mouth slants for a few microseconds and the eyes slightly roll.

How can you tell apart a genuine smile from a fake one? Pay close attention to the region around the person's eyes. If someone is genuinely happy, their smile invariably reaches their eye and causes the skin around the eyes to crinkle slightly. There are folds around the corner of the person's eyes if they are genuinely happy. Another clear sign of a genuine smile is a crow's feet formation just under the person's eyes. A smile is often used by people to hide their true feelings and emotions. It is near impossible to fake a smile (which is so involuntary and subconscious driven).

Even the direction of a person's chin can reveal a lot about their thoughts or personality. If their chin is jutting out, he/she may be a stubborn or obstinate about their stand.

Posture

When a person maintains an upright, well-aligned and relaxed posture, he/she is most likely in control of their thoughts and feelings and is confident/self-assured. Their shoulders don't slouch awkwardly, and the overall posture doesn't sag. On the other hand, a sagging posture can be a sign of low self-esteem or confidence. It can also mean placing yourself below others or subconsciously begging for sympathy.

When a person occupies too much space physically by sitting with their legs apart or broadening their shoulders, they are establishing their dominance or power by occupying more physical space.

Limbs

Pay close attention to people's limb movements when you are reading them. When a person is bored, disinterested, nervous or frustrated, they will fidget with an object or their fingers. Crossing arms is a big signal of being, closed, suspicious, uninspired or in disagreement with what you are saying. The person isn't receptive to what you are speaking about.

If you want to get the person to listen to what you are saying, open them up subconsciously first by changing the topic of conversation. Once they are in a more receptive state of mind, resume the topic. When a person crosses their arms or legs, they are less likely to absorb or be persuaded by what you say.

A person's handshake can reveal a great deal about what they think about themselves or their equation with the other person. For instance, a weak handshake is a sign of nervousness, low self-esteem, lack of confidence, submissiveness and uncertainty. Similarly, a crushing handshake can be an indication of dominance or aggressiveness. A firm handshake implies self-confidence and a sense of self-assuredness.

Observe the direction in which a person's feet are pointed. If they are pointed in your direction, it means the person is interested in what you are saying. On the other hand, if they are pointed away from you, the person is looking for an escape route. Feet pointing in your direction or leaning slightly towards you are huge non-verbal signals of attraction.

Legendary Hollywood talent scouting agent once famously uttered, "I don't have a contract with my clients. Just a handshake is enough." You can indeed tell volumes about a person simply through their handshake.

Tone

The tone of a person's voice can communicate a lot about the way a person is feeling or thinking. Look for any inconsistency in a person's tone. Does the tone and pitch vary throughout the conversation? This can be a signal that the person is experiencing a surge of emotions. Listen to the volume of a person's voice. Something may not be quite right if they are speaking in a softer or louder than usual manner. Observe if the person is using filler words rather than concise phrases or sentences. It can be a sign of nervousness or they may be buying time to make up stories.

A person's tone can convey emotions they try to conceal or are unable to express. They may say something flattering to you but their tone may be slightly sarcastic or bitter, which can be a giveaway to what they are truly feeling. It can indicate a more passive aggressive personality. The meaning of exactly the same words can change drastically when delivered using a different tone, volume and inflection.

Let's say the person ends their sentence on a higher note. Doesn't it sound more like a question than a definitive statement? Similarly, if the person finishes their sentence on a flat note, he/she is making a confident or assured statement.

The former can indicate doubt, uncertainty or suspicion, while the latter can be an indication of authority.

Proxemics

Proxemics refers to the physical space maintained during communication between people, which reveals volumes about how they relate to each other. Haven't you experienced a feeling of discomfort when someone tried to invade your personal space or come closer than you appreciate? This person is most likely seeking acceptance from you or trying to make their way into your inner social circle.

On the other hand, if a person comes closer than intended during negotiations, he/she may be trying to intimidate you or subconscious coax you into accepting their conditions. The ideal distance to test a person's comfort level is to stand at a minimum distance of four feet from them. If the person appears open, they are welcoming into their personal space. Similarly, if they are rigid, don't jump into their personal space immediately. They may not be ready to include you into their personal zone.

Mirroring

Mirroring a person's body language is a wonderful way to establish a rapport with a person on a subconscious level. Closely observe a person's body language while they are interacting with you. How is their posture? What are the words they typically use? If they are leaning against the bar or table, follow suit. Similarly, if they sip on their drink, mirror their action. If you spot them resting their elbow on a table, mirror their action.

Mirroring a person's action gives the other person an impression that you are one among them. It works on a primordial level to create sense of affiliation, likeliness and belongingness even before spoken language was invented. Adapt your actions, posture, gesture and movements with the other person to give a feeling of "being one among them." If the person is following your actions, they are seeking acceptance or validation from you.

Chapter Three: Reading People Through Personality Types

Personality analysis is a field that is constantly evolving and varied. There are varying schools of psychological thoughts and theories when it comes to studying an individual's personality. Some of the most popular personality analyzing schools include trait theory, social learning, biological/genetic personality influencer and more.

Personality refers to an individual's distinct characteristics connected to processing thoughts, feelings and emotions that eventually determine their behavior. It involves taking into consideration all the traits a person possess to understand them as an entity. Personality study also includes understanding the inherent differences existing between people where particular characteristics are concerned.

Here are some of the most common personality type classifications.

Type A, B, C and D

Type A personality people are at a bigger risk of contracting heart diseases since they are known to be more aggressive, competitive, ambitious, short-tempered, impatient, impulsive and hyper active. Type A personality theory was introduced in the 50's by Meyer Friedman and Ray Rosenman. These people are more stressed due to their constant need to accomplish a lot. They are always striving to be better than others, which invariably leads to greater anxiety and stress.

Type B people are more reflective, balanced, even-tempered, inventive and less competitive by personality. They experience less stress and anxiety, along with staying unaffected by competition or time constraints. A Type B personality person is moderately ambitious and lives more in the present. They have a steadier and more restrained disposition. Type B folks are social, modest, innovative, gentle mannered, relaxed and low on stress.

Later psychologists came up with other personality types, too, since they found the division into Type A and B more restrictive. They discovered that some people demonstrated a combination of both A and B Type traits. Thus, segregating people into only two distinct personality groups doesn't do justice to the classification. This lead to the creation of even more personality types!

Type C people have a more meticulous eye for detail. They are focused, curious and diplomatic. There tend to put other people's needs before theirs. They are seldom assertive, straightforward and opinionated. This leads to Type C folks developing pent up resentment, frustration, anxiety and depression. There is a propensity to take everything seriously, which makes them reliable and efficient workers.

This personality type also possess high analytic skills, logical thinking powers and intelligence. However, they need to develop the knack of learning to be less diplomatic and more assertive. Type C also needs to develop the ability to relax and let their hair down periodically.

Lastly, Type D personality people are known to hold a more pessimistic view of life. They are socially awkward and withdrawn, and do not enjoy being in the limelight. They are constantly worried about being rejected by people. Type D people are at a greater risk of suffering from mental illnesses such as depression owing to pessimism, pent up frustration and melancholy. Since the Type D personality doesn't share things easily with others, they suffer internally.

Psychoanalytic Theory

This theory is different from the regular personality classification theories in the sense that the analysis is based is not based on the responses of people about their personality, but a more in-depth study of people's personalities by glimpsing into their subconscious or unconscious mind. Since the analysis is based on a study on a person's subconscious mind, errors and instances of misleading the reader are eliminated.

In psychoanalysis, a person's words and actions are known to be disguised manifestations for their underlying subconscious emotions. The founding father of the psychoanalytic theory was Sigmund Freud, who was of the view that all human behavior is primarily driven by primitive instincts, passions, impulse and underlying emotions. He theorized that all human behavior is a direct consequence of the equation between our id, ego and superego.

Through the free association method that includes experiences, memories, dreams and more; Freud analyzed underlying emotions, thoughts and feelings that determine their attitude and behavior. Thus a majority of our behavior can be traced to our early childhood experiences that are still lingering in our subconscious mind, which we may or may not be aware of.

For example, if an individual demonstrates aggressive traits as an adult, it can be pinned down to the violence, harassment or bullying he/she experienced in their early childhood. Similarly, if a child comes from an environment where there were very high expectations from him/her and the parents were seldom happy with his/her accomplishments, he/she may constantly seek validation or acceptance from others. They may fear rejection.

Thus, a person's childhood experiences can help you determine their personality and read them even more effectively according to the psychoanalytic theory. The theory is still extensively used when it comes to helping people cope with depression, anger, stress, panic attacks, aggression, obsessive disorders and much more.

Carl Jung's Personality Classification Theory

Psychologist Carl Jung classified people on the basis on their sociability quotient into introverts and extroverts. Introverts are folks who are primarily inward driven, shy, withdrawn and reticent. They are more focused on their ideas and sensibilities than the external world around them. Introverts are known to be more logical, reflective and sensible by nature. They take time to crawl out of their box, and establish a rapport with others.

On the other hand, extroverts are outgoing, friendly, affable, social and gregarious people who live more in the present than worry about the future. They have a more positive and exuberant disposition, and are more than willing to accept challenges or changes.

After classifying people as introverts and extroverts, Jung received his share of brickbats from psychologists who believed that the classification was too restrictive to categorize every human being on the planet. Experts argued that a majority of people rarely demonstrated extreme introvert or extrovert tendencies. According to them only a majority of people possess extreme introvert or extrovert tendencies. Most people in fact possess a little bit of both, and their behavior differs according to the situation.

For instance, someone like me enjoys going out and spending time with people but I also value some time alone for reflection and contemplation every now and then. This neither makes me a hardcore extrovert or introvert but more of a combination of both – an ambivert.

Social Learning

This theory talks about how people pick up personality or behavioral traits from their immediate environment. It proposes that an individual's behavior is a result of their growing up conditions and environment. We pick up specific patterns and personality traits through our experiences. Social learning psychologists are of the view that all our behavior is learnt through our social experiences.

For example, if a person has been rewarded in a specific manner, he or she learns behavior through positive reinforcement and experiences. For example, someone throwing excessive tantrums may have learned through their experiences that drama gets them attention. Every time they want attention they know throwing tantrums will do the trick. At times, we don't have to experience something to learn behavior. Our mind is conditioned to use complex codes, information, actions, symbols and consequences. A majority of our observations and vicarious experiences drive our behavior, and help us imbibe specific personality traits.

Ernest Kretschmer's Classification

German psychologist Ernest Kretschmer's personality classification theory theorizes that a person's physical characteristics or personality traits determine the likelihood of a person suffering from mental ailments and their personality.

According to this personality classification, people are classified as Athletic, Pyknic, Dysplastic and Asthenic. Pyknic personality types are people who are round, stout and short. They demonstrate more extrovert traits such as gregariousness, friendliness and an outgoing disposition.

The Aesthetic personality types are people who have a slender and slim appearance. They have a fundamentally introvert personality. These are folks who have strong, athletic and robust bodies, and demonstrate more aggressive, enthusiastic and energetic characteristics.

Briggs Myers Personality Indicator

There are multiple personality tests that determine an individual's personality type based on a psychological analysis. One of the most widely used personality analysis tests is the Briggs Myers Personality Indicator. It is a comprehensive report that analyzes people's personalities based on how they perceive the world and make decisions.

The Briggs-Myers Personality Indictor was created by Isabel Briggs Myers and Katherine Briggs. It is based on Jung's theory but expounds on it through four primary psychological functions or processes such as sensation, thinking, feeling and intuition.

The MBTI emphasizes on one of the four primary functions dominating over other traits. The personality indicator operates on an assumption that everyone possesses a preference for the manner in which they experience the world around them. These inherent differences emphasize our values, motives, beliefs and interests, and thus determine an overall personality.

There are around 16 distinct personality types based on this psychological personality analysis theory. The Briggs-Myers test comprises several questions, where test respondents reveal their personality through their answers. This test is also widely used in areas such as determining a person's chances of success in a particular role and compatibility in interpersonal relationships.

In Myers Briggs personality theory, a personality type is determined when there is a clear preference for one style over another. Different letters connected with individual preferences helps determine the person's Myers Briggs personality type. For instance, if a person reveals a clear tendency for I, S, T and J, they have the ISTJ personality type.

Extraversion and introversion – The first letter of the Briggs-Myers personality type is related to the direction of one's energy. If a person is externally focused or focused on the external world, they show a preference for extraversion. On the contrary, if the energy is inward directed, the person shows a clear inclination for introversion.

Sensing and Intuition – The second letter is concerned with processing information. If an individual prefers dealing with information, has clarity, can describe what they see etc. then they show a distinct preference for sensing. Intuition, on the other hand, is related to intangible ideas and concepts. Intuition is represented by the letter "N."

Thinking and Feeling – The third letter reflects an individual's decision making personality. People who show an inclination for analytic, logical and detached thinking reveal a tendency for thinking over feeling. Similarly, people who show a preference for feeling are more driven by their values or what they believe in.

Judgment and Perception – The last letter of the Briggs-Myer Type Indicator shows a person's way of viewing the world. If an individual reveals a preference for going with the tide and he/she is more flexible in their approach towards responding to things as they arise, they are perception driven. However, if their thoughts are more planned, rigid and clearly structured, they show an inclination for judging (judgment).

1. **INTJ – Introverted, Intuitive, Thinking and Judging**

   The INTJ personality type is primarily inventive, strategic, imaginative, resourceful and creative. They have a clear plan for everything. They are known to be original, analytical, independent thinking and resolute. They are good at planning, and executing plans into action. The INTJ personality type is perceptive when it comes to recognizing patterns and giving a clear logical reason for patterns.

   They have a high sense of responsibility and commitment, and rarely quit something without completing it. They have high expectations not just from themselves but others too. The INTJ personality type makes for wonderful leaders, and also dedicated followers. These are generally the kind of people you want as original and independent thinking leaders.

2. ISTJ – Introverted, Sensing, Thinking, Judging

ISTJs are composed, quiet, reserved, serious and contemplative. They are primarily focused on living a secure, unruffled and peaceful life. These people are highly reliable, meticulous, disciplined, responsible and precision-oriented. They are logical, rational and practical. ISTJ folks possess a steady approach when it comes to fulfilling their objectives.

There is a deep respect for position, authority, establishment and a more conventional way of living. ISTJ people are concerned about maintaining order in their immediate physical space, work and life. If you are looking for administrators or managers for your business, these people may be a good fit.

3. ISFJ – Introverted, Sensing, Feeling, Judging

ISFJ people are quiet, kind, responsible conscientious. They are focused on fulfilling their responsibilities and obligations. There is a clear tendency for being practical, balanced and steady. They have an inherent need to place the feelings and needs of other people over theirs. ISFJ personality type people lean towards conventions and established norms. They don't believe in challenging customers, and are more concerned about leading a peaceful and secure life.

The ISFJ personality type is intuitively tuned in to the needs, emotions and feelings of other people. They have a deep service sense, and are suitable for vocations where they are needed to be of help to other people.

4. ESTJ – Extroverted, Sensing, Thinking and Judging

ESTJ people live in the moment, and have a high sense of appreciation for the present moment. They demonstrate a high sense of reverence for conventions, traditions and established customs, and they'll rarely go against it. ESTJ folks have a good idea about how things should be resolved speedily and effectively. This makes them a good fit for leadership positions. They are logical, rational, practical and innately realistic.

The ESTJ personality type excels at managing complex projects, and is focused on completing things with careful attention to details. They are reliable and dependable when it comes to accomplishing challenging tasks. The ESTJ personality type put in a lot into each task they undertake, which makes them efficient project managers or leaders. They place a lot of premium on law, justice, social order and security.

5. **ISTP – Introverted, Sensing, Thinking and Perceiving**

ISTP type people are inquisitive, curious and intelligent people who are always focused on knowing how everything works. They demonstrate a composed, peaceful and unruffled disposition. ISTP people also possess highly developed motor/mechanical skills and show an inclination for intense adventure. These people are more tolerant, flexible and adaptive by nature. They are excellent observers, people watchers and analyzers. ISTP folks are known to dive into the base of any situation before they come up with an actionable solution.

They will almost always emphasize on organizing facts, and establishing a precise cause and effect relationship. These are almost always the problem solvers, analyzers or solution providers that appear more logical and emotionally detached. Their solutions are more logically driven and less determined by emotions.

6. ISFP – Introverted, Sensing, Feeling, Perceiving

ISFP personality type people are shy, reflective, kind and sensitive. They avoid confrontation, arguments or heated conflict, and always focus on forming peaceful and harmonious relationships. ISFP people will avoid situations where there is scope for conflict. One distinct characteristic is the ISFP type's evolved sense of aesthetics. There is a higher tendency to be broadminded, adaptive and accommodating.

The ISFP folks aren't obstinate about their views, and posses a high sense of balance and appreciation for other people's views. They will agree to disagree with others in a graceful manner. ISFP type people are inventive, independent thinking and path-breaking original. They safeguard their space fiercely, and attempt to work within the given time frame with diligence. They live for the moment, and aren't too worked up about their future.

7. ESTP – Extroverted, Sensing, Thinking, Perceiving

ESTP personality type are outgoing folks who use a more rational, practical and logical approach while handling challenges. They focus on gaining fast results and solutions. ESTP people very efficient when it comes to analyzing people through multiple clues! They make for excellent psychologists, investigators and people analyzers. They are intuitive, and pick on both verbal and non-verbal clues effectively.

The ESTP personality type is action-oriented and practical, and prefers tangible actions over intangible ideas. They have a more problem solving, energetic, enthusiastic and proactive approach to life. They ESTP type people are more spontaneous, focused, random and attentive. Their ideal learning approach is hands on knowledge or learning by doing. They seek solutions by actively taking their problems head-on.

8. ESFP – Extroverted, Sensing, Feeling, Perceiving

ESTP type people are gregarious, flexible, amiable, loving and contemplative by nature. They seek new experiences, alternatives and possibilities. This personality type is also open for figuring out new ways to do things. They also like unique, unusual and off-beat stuff. These people are high on positivity and optimism.

They also make for exceptionally good team members, and love to combine their skills with other people to accomplish great results. These are folks who believe in living life queen or king size, while also developing solid relationships with others. The ESFP type is not very good when it comes to handling expectation, pressure and stress. They become pessimistic, negative and insecure.

9. ENTJ – Extroverted, Intuitive, Thinking and Judging

The ENTJ personality type is forthright, straightforward and outspoken, which makes them excellent leaders. According to them, the world is full of possibilities. Rather than perceiving problems as hurdles, they view them as challenges. ENTJ personality type people are ambitious, practical, career-minded and solution oriented.

They will consider problems from several angles before coming up with practical, effective and workable solutions. The ENTJ personality type is in its element when it comes to goal setting and fulfilling these goals. The ENTJ personality type are outspoken, clear decision makers and effortless leaders. For these people, the world is full of possibilities.

They are well-read, knowledgeable, abreast with what is happening in the world and more aggressive when it comes to expressing their ideas. While they may not be too intuitively connected to other people's feelings, ENTJs can be surprisingly emotional.

10.   INFP – Introverted, Intuitive, Feeling and Perceiving

The INFP personality type folks are balanced, composed, calm and contemplative. They are fiercely loyal and true to their value system. These people care deeply about others. They have a strong belief and value system, which guides them while making important decisions. The INFP people are loyal, adjusting, reliable, adaptable to change and relaxed. They easily empathize with other people, and reach to other people to make things easier for them.

11. **INTP – Introvert, Intuitive, Thinking, Perceiving**

INTP type people are independent thinking, creative, logical and analytic. They have a high sense of respect for knowledge and skills. By nature, they are reserved, reticent and withdrawn. They tend to exist in a world of their own and show little inclination for following others. The INTP personality type is fiercely independent and individualistic. They believe in creating their own route rather than following the one set by others.

12. **ENFJ – Extroverted, Intuitive, Feeling and Judging**

The ENFJ people have inherently well-developed people skills, and are known to be empathetic, kind, disciplined and affectionate. They are more externally focused and seldom enjoy being by themselves. The ENFJ people demonstrate an exceptional ability for spotting talent and skills in people. They also go out of the way to help people fulfill their real potential, thus making them wonderful leaders and managers.

One of the ENFJ personality type's best trait is their ability to accept praise and criticism with equal ease, while being faithful to people.

13. ESFJ – Extroverted, Sensing, Feeling and Judging

They ESFJ personality type are people who thrive when they are in the midst of other people. They are people persons, who enjoy interacting with other people, developing meaningful relationships with them, and getting to know them well. There is a huge need to be liked, admired and accepted by others. The ESFJ personality type desires that everything around them should be positive, balanced and harmonious for which they may go all out to support other people.

ESFJ people possess an inherent knack when it comes to making other people feel good about themselves. They will compliment and praise people lavishly in public, and ensure their strengths are highlighted. This personality type is popular because they have an inherent ability to make others feel special.

Their value or belief system is primarily guided by people around them, which makes them less rigid when it comes to their value system and beliefs. Also, they are more flexible when it comes to their different situations and persons. The ESFJ type enjoy being appreciated and are in their element when it comes to contributing to mankind's welfare. In any situation, they are concerned about the greater good.

14. ENTP – Extroverted, Intuitive, Thinking and Perceiving

The ENTP personality type is excited by ideas and concepts. They are able to analyze people and situations instinctively. They are fast decision makers and action takers. ENTP type people are also more alert, guarded, forthright and attentive. They are more fixated on possibilities or alternatives than plans.

They are excellent conversationalists who leave everyone bewitched with their words. ENTP don't like sticking to a routine, and are constantly seeking new experiences. They are experts at reading people, and have a deep sense of respect for learning. Again, they will consider multiple possibilities before zeroing down on a single solution.

15. ENFP – Extroverted, Intuitive, Feeling and Perceiving

The ENFP personality type people are fiercely independent, original and individualistic by nature. They believe in creating their own unique methods, habits, ideas, concepts and actions. This personality type doesn't fancy interacting with cookie clutter folks who follow the herd. They also despise being constrained in a box.

The ENFP personality type enjoys being around others and possess a strong sense of intuitive and sensitivity for others as well as themselves. They are more driven by emotions, and are known to be perceptive and contemplative. The ENFP personality type will think deeply about things from an emotional perspective before making a decision.

ENFP people are capable of accomplishing success in tasks that interest them. However, they also have a tendency to get easily bored doing things they aren't really good at. They don't fare too well when it comes to jobs that involve more meticulous, routine and detail-oriented tasks. They thrive in professions that allow them to express their creativity and come up with innovative ideas. Positions that are more confining and boxed will not appeal to them.

16. INFJ – Introverted, Intuitive, Feeling and Judging

The INFJ personality type are idealists, observers and visionaries who thrive on ideas and imagination. They have a unique and profound way of viewing the world. This personality type has the tendency to look at the world on a substantial and in-depth manner. They will seldom accept things as they are. While others view the INFJ personality as weird or eccentric, they stick to their unusual views about life.

The INFJ people are compassionate, caring, gentle and complex individuals who are more inclined towards creative, independent and artistic endeavors. They reside in a world that filled esoteric possibilities. While this personality type places a high premium of order and organization, they can also be surprisingly spontaneous and intuitive.

They will be able understand ideas intuitively without pinpointing the reason. This makes the

INFJ people less organized and systematic than other judging personality types.

Chapter Four: Effectively Analyzing People Through Their Words

We don't use words mindlessly. There is a reason (often subconscious) behind our choice of words. The words we use are often guided by our subconscious feelings, emotions and thoughts. There is a clear underlying meaning behind phrases, words and other verbal expressions. Let us say for example, a person tells you that "Oh, so now you are dating another doctor." What does their choice of the word "another" indicate? It may imply that you just got out of a terrible relationship with a doctor, and fool hardily started dating another.

People use "yeah" and other similar terms when they want to communicate ambivalence. Similarly, they use "dude", "sis" or "bro" to express solidarity with people. It can be a sign of loyalty or friendship. There may also be a deep-seated need to be liked or accepted by the other person. People using these terms may seek to establish a sense of familiarity and belongingness with others. Begin by closely observing people's words and use it for peeking into the mind to unveil the thoughts and emotions behind their expressions.

Watch Out For Adjectives and Adverbs

The human brain is no short of a marvel. It is incredibly effective when it comes to thinking and vocalizing thoughts and/or ideas. When we think, our brains primarily use verbs and nouns. However, when we convert ideas or thoughts into language, we tend to elaborate on our thoughts by using adverbs and adjectives. These adverbs and adjectives that we use for describing basic nouns and verbs can reveal a lot about our inner feelings, thoughts and emotions. They can also offer a glimpse into our predominant values, and other ideas.

For example, let us consider a sentence such as "I ate". It comprises a pronoun and action verb. The words or expressions used to modify these sentences can offer plenty of information about a person. These are modifying words that give clues into an individual's value system or behavioral patterns. Through verbal expressions or clues, you can make a fairly reliable guess about an individual's state of mind or character. If you add "fast" to the above sentence, it indicates urgency.

They may eat fast because they are late for a meeting or are conscious about being punctual. It can reveal a more commitment-driven, responsible, dedicated and disciplined approach. They have a deep sense of respect for social norms, and may be focused on other's expectations. They may be your ideal employees since they are fast, punctual and committed. Of course, there can be plenty of other reasons why a person eats fast. However, descriptive words can offer you a good indication about people's thoughts, behavior and overall values.

Read Between the Lines

Not everything people say reveals a lot about them. Often, what they leave unsaid also says a lot about them. Even when someone offers you a compliment such as "You are looking cool today", it may not go down well with you. To you it may imply that you are looking cool only today and not every day. We subconsciously tune in to what is left unsaid.

Let us take another example to understand the hidden meaning behind words or what people leave unsaid. You take your friends out a newly opened restaurant in your neighborhood. It's a much talked about place and you just can't wait to try the stuff there. As soon as you enter, the waiter/server greets you warmly and directs your group to the table.

What follows is an elaborate seven course meal. Before serving you each of the scrumptious courses, the waiter introduces each course and tells you interesting details about the preparations. You have a great time wining and dining with friends. Once you finish the entire seven course meal, you request the waiter to bring your check.

The waiter brings over your check and asks you for your feedback about the food. You sum it up in a single line by stating, "The soup was good." The waiter doesn't react too positively and looks a tad disappointed. You wonder why! According to you, you just paid him/her a compliment. However, the things you left unsaid revealed a lot about your opinion or thoughts regarding the food.

The other person subconsciously latched on to what you left unsaid. It revealed that apart from the soup, nothing else was worth mentioning or everything other than the soup was average. While people communicate plenty through what they say, they leave a lot of things unsaid.

I Test

This is yet another verbal determinant of an individual's personality. If a person uses the term "I" excessively, it indicates self-centeredness, selfishness or a large ego. However, the more "I" a person uses, the less powerful he/she feels. People who aren't sure about their power feel the desire to establish false sense of power through excessive usage of "I." Do a tiny exercise right now. Browse through the mails that are sent by people in a position of high authority. Now compare these mails will people who aren't in very authoritative positions, you'll clearly notice more usage of "I" in the latter.

For example, "Dear Jones, I was a student of your biology class last year. I have always enjoyed being a part of your classes. I've learned a lot through them. I received an email from you related to research collaboration. I would really appreciate working with you." Mr. Jones may reply with "That's amazing news. This week may be slightly busy for me owing to prior commitments. How about a meeting next Tuesday from 5 to 7? It will be wonderful to catch up."

Other than an indication of less power and higher self consciousness, it is also a clue of depression. A research published in Scientific Study of Literature revealed that illustrious poets who committed suicide frequently resorted to the usage of first-person pronouns while writing poetry.

Talking About Others

What people say about other people is often a reflection of their own personality. In a research conducted by Siminie Vazire and Peter Harms, it has been discovered that asking people to rate others on three negative and three positive aspects gave plenty of insights about their social personality, overall being, mental health and their view about others. It was found that a person's tendency to see others in a more positive light indicates their own positivity.

There is a powerful link between having an opinion about other people and possessing an energetic, courteous, optimistic, emotionally balanced and kind personality. Talking positively about other people demonstrates how positively they view their own lives. On the other hand, people who use unflattering and negative words and phrases view themselves in an inferior light.

There is a greater correlation between using unflattering words used for describing other people and narcissism, low self-confidence, anti-social tendencies, frustration, overall dissatisfaction and more. People with a primarily negative personality type tend to view others in a more unflattering light. This can be a strong indication of mental issues, personality disorder or an unstable mind.

The Object Description Analysis

The manner in which a person describes an object is also enough to give you a fair idea about how the individual views the world, along with how he/she thinks and feels. The most commonly used cluster words will offer a clear basis for their behavior and personality. This linguistic personality determination technique is called meaning extraction.

Additional Words

The extra or additional words a person uses while conversing with you can reveal a lot about their thoughts, behavior and personality. For example, if someone says, "I won yet another award" in place of "I won an award", it reveals a need to tell people that they've won plenty of awards earlier. The individual may be struck with a terrible complex that makes them scream about their objection from rooftops.

Pick up this clue and learn that one of the best ways to develop a rapport with this person is to hail them for their accomplishments. Their words present an area of weakness that you can quickly cash on. Watch out for an incompatibility between the person's verbal and non-verbal clues. For example, an individual may state that they are delighted to meet you. However, if their body language is rigid, inflexible and uncomfortable, something may be wrong. A trained eye can easily figure out inconsistencies between a person's verbal and non-verbal signals.

You can fall back on their words and body language collectively to understand what the person is thinking or feeling.

"I Made Up My Mind" – Introverts and Extroverts

If an individual says he/she has made up their mind, they have most likely considered several options before making a clear decision. It implies that a person is prone to contemplating and reflecting upon their decision rather than making spur of the moment decisions. They have deliberated on their decision, and may be analytic or logical by nature.

There are lesser chances of them being rash, spontaneous and impulsive decision makers. The words are an indication of a person's introvertedness and extrovertedness. Taking decisions after giving it a thought is a sign of introvertedness.

However, guard against making instant, sporadic decisions about people based on the words they use. Simply using "decided" or "I made up my mind" isn't enough to make conclusions about an individual's personality. Identify a clear pattern and several verbal/non-verbal clues to read people more effectively. Watch out for clues that support your initial reading or point to contrary evidence.

Extroverts collect their energies from other people and their environment. They stimulation and decision making comes from using the trial and error technique over reflectively contemplating on their decision. Extroverts may speak more spontaneously without thinking, while introverts will carefully weight their words and its implications.

You can tailor your own communication pattern to suit the other person's once you get to know if they are an introvert or extrovert. Identifying whether a person is an introvert or extrovert helps you understand how someone makes decisions. For example, let us say you are selling insurance. You may have to determine what drives both the introvert and extrovert personality types to make a decision about buying insurance.

Introverts may be more reflective and mull over the options before making a decision, while extroverts are more prone to making quick decisions. If you notice a primarily introverted mindset, give people more time to think before making a decision. Pushing these folks to make a quick decision may backfire. They may get uncomfortable with the idea of being pushed into a decision.

If you are negotiating important businesses deals, you don't give introverts enough time to mull over the conditions, they may come up with a negative response. On the contrary, people who make fast decisions show sign of being extroverts. They can be pushed into making fast decisions. However, one of the most vital things to keep in mind is that people rarely demonstrate absolute introvert or extrovert tendencies. A majority of people are a combination of introvertedness and extrovertedness.

Chapter Five: Personality and Birth Order

An individual's birth order can also reveal a lot of his or her personality. This isn't just restricted to pop psychology talk or mindless party chatter but based on a psychological analysis of how the person relates to their family members and how they are treated within the family based on their position or birth order. A person's family dynamics plays a considerable role in shaping their personality. The role they fulfilled as children or during their adolescent years influences their behavior as adults. Our status quo as children establishes the foundation for our actions as adults. Notice how several times children born in the same family or raised in the same environment have dramatically diverse personalities.

Of course, there are other factors that in combination with a person's birth order can determine their personality type. These factors such as the family's overall socio-economic status, education, number of children in the family, parent's professional achievements and more also impacts an individual's personality.

It was Alfred Adler who first came up with the theory of studying an individual's personality through their birth rank. He used it a method for reading the behavior, personality and actions of his clients. However, it was Frank Sulloway who elaborated on the theory in his publication *Born to Rebel*. Sulloway's book identified five primary traits like extraversion, agreeableness, neuroticism, consciousness and openness.

The psychologist mentioned that an individual's birth order impacts their personality even more than their environment. This means that the chances of two first-borns having the same personality type is higher than two children belonging to one family.

Here are some ways to read a person through their birth order.

First-borns

First born children are known to be responsible and ambitious leaders, who pave the way for others. They are original, creative and independent thinking by nature. Since they get more undivided attention and time with their parents, they have a clear edge over their siblings. Again, they are more proactive and take the lead when it comes to caring for the siblings, which makes them more disciplined, inspiring, responsible and accountable as adults. They are protective towards those weaker than them, and often lead others.

If parents place a lot of expectations on the first in a household, the person may grow up feeling inadequate. This may not just lead to low self esteem but also a weak personality that is marked by a constant need for validation, acceptance and approval. The person may end up feeling that they can never be good enough for anything.

First born individuals are more goal-oriented and ambitious. They give plenty of importance to accomplishments and success. They thrive in or perform well in positions of authority, responsibility and maintaining discipline. There is an inherent tendency to be a control freak, while also being autocratic, dictatorial and bossy.

Owing to the fact that come first in the sibling hierarchy, these people are physically stronger than other children in the household, which gives them a marked dominant personality. They may have a high sense of entitlement.

First-borns are often high on determination, rule enforcement and attention to details.

Middle-borns

Since they are caught between two siblings, middle-borns develop a more complicated personality. They are neither given the rights and responsibilities of the older sibling nor the special privileges of the youngest sibling. This makes them look outside the home for friendships and connections.

Middle-borns often have very big social circles and are known to be excellent diplomats and negotiators. They are social creatures who function with a profound sense of peace and fairness. Middle-borns are fiercely loyal to their loves ones and seldom betray people's trust. Typical personality traits of middle born children are flexibility, generosity and adaptability. They are known for their diplomatic nature, and can play peacemakers in any situation.

Middle born children are primarily understanding, co-operative and adjusting. They also turn out to be competitive adults. Middle-borns have a close-knit social circle who award them the affection they haven't received within their family. Middle-borns are late raisers, and discover their calling after plenty of experimentation, contemplation and deliberation. They are at the center of authoritative careers that allow them to utilize their power-packed negotiation skills.

Middle-borns are generally social and operate with a deep sense of justice and fairness. Their typical personality characteristics include generosity, diplomacy, flexibility and adaptability. They are good at teamwork, and relate well with people belonging to multiple personality types since they have learnt to deal with older and younger siblings. Middle-borns display a more affable nature, and they know how to wriggle themselves out of confrontations and conflicts. They are known to be resourceful and quickly master multiple skills.

Last Born

By the time the youngest child of the family is born, parents are well-versed in their parenting skills and more economically settled. This makes them less paranoid and more secure. They aren't excessively monitored, which makes them more independent and freedom. Last born are excellent decision makers, and operate with a high sense of entitlement.

The last born is known to be charming and risk taking. They are independent thinking, original and adventurous. There is a greater tendency to rewrite the rules rather than following set norms.

Parents are less careful when it comes to their last born because they've already experienced being a parent, which helps them give more leeway and flexibility to the youngest child. Also, there are higher chances of pampering and indulging the child owing to a better financial status. Since parents are more relaxed and lenient with last-borns, they don't turn out to be conformists. They are used to plenty of attention, and they don't worship authority.

Rather than walking on set paths, they will create their own path. Since they've learnt to compete with their siblings for their parent's time and attention, they are good are handling competition and aren't easily bothered by feelings of envy and insecurity.

Since they are more creative and independent thinking, they thrive in careers such as stand up comedians, painters, dancers and authors. Typical personality characteristics include empathy, obstinacy, extroversion, manipulativeness, penchant for drama and more. These are your salespeople, since they are glib and can talk themselves of almost any situation.

Sole Child

The only child doesn't have to complete with anyone for their parents' time and attention, which makes them self-centered. There is a tendency to think that everything revolves around them. They tend to spend a lot of time alone, which turns them into more original, resourceful, inventive and creative people. Sole or only children find new and innovative ways to keep themselves busy. By nature, they are more confident, self-assured, meticulous, expressive and firm. They express their opinions more assertively and confidently.

Since they do not have to deal with sibling rivalry of any kind, they are always used to having things their way. They become edgy and unsettled when they have to complete with others or things don't go their way. Sole-borns find it tough to share the limelight with others. They almost always want to be the center of attention since they've never had to complete with any for attention at home through their childhood and adolescent years. Only-borns are constantly seeking attention, respect and attention. In the absence of siblings as role models, their only role models are elders of the house. Since grown-ups become their role models, they grow up to be perfectionists.

There are multiple factors that impact a person's behavioral characteristics and personality. To make a more accurate reading an individual's personality through birth order, there are some effective tips offers by psychologists. They recommend analyzing a person's siblings while reading their personality since no two children in the same household ever share the same role. If one assumes the role of a caretaker, the other will invariably be the care recipient.

Other factor that are taken into consideration while analyzing an individual's personality through birth order is genetics, gender, social status and other factors (apart from their birth order). These factors together will help you make more accurate readings about an individual's personality than simply relying on birth order.

Conclusion

I genuinely hope this book has offered you multiple invaluable insights about reading people's personality through well-researched strategies, tried and tested techniques and a bunch of practical tips. These tips can be applied in just about any situation from professional to interpersonal relationships to your social life.

Whether you want to figure out the personality of a prospective buyer during a negotiation or the personality traits of the new date you have your eyes on, this book is a valuable resource for helping you read others effectively. If there's a single largest skill that translates into success in modern times, it is the knack of reading people.

When you know how a person thinks or feels, you can mould your message according to his or her personality for accomplishing an optimally beneficial outcome.

The next step is to use this book and apply it in your everyday life in tiny, gradual ways to start with. Begin by observing people at the airport, supermarket or doctor's clinic when you have free time. You'll become more interested in the art of analyzing people, and find yourself doing it at every given opportunity.

Finally, if you enjoyed reading the book, please take the time to share your views by posting a review of Amazon. It'd be highly appreciated!

How to Analyze People 2

Rapid Deduction Techniques To Think And Analyze People Like Sherlock Holmes

Patrick Lightman

104

Introduction

Imagine possessing the ability to decipher within a couple of meetings if a prospective date has it in him or her to be a supportive, compatible and inspiring long-term partner. Imagine telling through a potential client's verbal and nonverbal clues if he or she will negotiate on your terms. Imagine being able to decode though a prospective buy's clues if he or she is likely to buy from you. Is a business associate satisfied with your terms and conditions to go ahead with a deal? Is the salesperson trying to mislead you into buying or are they speaking the truth? Can you read people's reactions to steer the communication in a favorable direction?

This is the power of being able to analyze people's reactions. You can predetermine the outcomes of different communication styles and adapt the one that suits the other person the most to accomplish a beneficial outcome.

Plenty of conflicts we experience in our daily lives are entrenched in our inability to read or analyze other people accurate. We fail to understand how they are thinking and feeling, which creates misunderstandings. Then again, our inherent insecurities are all rooted in what people think about us. Will my partner cherish my existence in their life? Does he or she value me? Does my manager appreciate my skills? These are the most inherent fears that we operate with. Once we learn to read people, these insecurities and uncertainties don't bog us down.

Knowing how-to speed-read people accurately is nothing short of a superpower or secret magic weapon. Imagine possessing the superpower to quickly read a person like a book. You will be eliminating tiresome guesswork from relationships and focus on communicating with a person that is most suitable for his or her thoughts, feelings and personality.

When we learn to become more telepathic and master the knack of reading other people, we can use our cards in a manner that is beneficial for us. You don't have to develop the knack of being an FBI style investigator to analyze people or understand how they think and feel. All you need to do is watch out for verbal and non-verbal clues that the person is constantly giving out to know what they are thinking.

A person is consciously and subconsciously giving out plenty of clues about not just what they are currently thinking and feeling but also their overall personality, ideologies, values, attitude, preferences and much more. You only have to be perceptive enough to tune in these clues at a subconscious level.

I recently read a piece about how what the content you like on Facebook can help determine everything from your sexual preferences to gender to relationship status. Imagine, your social media likes determining your subconscious persona.

There are plenty of clues of everywhere; you just need to watch out for them.

Even when we don't realize, people are constantly giving away signals about how they are thinking and feeling. When you know exactly what to look for, your intuition, perceptiveness and subconscious communication increases multi-fold. At times, you don't understand people because you aren't actively tuning in to these signals. People are nothing short of an enigma and learning to watch out for the right clues allows you to put together prices of a challenging puzzle.

Our knack for analyzing people influences the manner through which we interact with them. When you understand how a person processes information and emotions, the message can be delivered in a manner that is most beneficial for everyone involved.

According to research conducted by MIT, the other person's body language is an accurate giveaway about the outcomes of the negotiation 80 percent of the time. This implies that the person is offering clues about their inner feelings and thoughts involuntarily almost all the while.

An individual's overall personality is a sum total of several attributes, including beliefs, learnt behavior, childhood experiences, gender roles, birth order, peer influence, genetics, environment and others. All these factors are noticeable in the way people speak and conduct themselves.

While a layperson may view people itching their nose as a seemingly harmless or reflex gesture, a people analyzer will always seek deeper meaning in the action.

For instance, if a person has been confronted with facts where their lies have been called out and they start scratching their nose, he or she may most likely be lying. These gestures happen at such a subconscious level that the person isn't even aware that they are sending out these signals or doing these gestures, which makes these verbal and non-clues almost impossible to fake. These gestures are directed by the subconscious mind and are more reflex actions than awareness driven behavior.

Research has it that a person retains around 10 percent of the information imparted verbally, and 20 percent of visually communicated information. However, we remember around 80 percent of the information that is conveyed using a combination of both verbal and non-verbal communication methods. This also means that if you combine both verbal and non-verbal communication clues, your chances of being an effective and persuasive communicator will increase.

Body language along with other non-verbal clues is important when it comes to analyzing people. When a person's non-verbal clues match their verbal clues, it is a sign of confidence, authenticity, trustworthiness and clarity. On the contrary, if there is a clear mismatch between a person's verbal and nonverbal clues, it can indicate mistrust, deceit and lies. The person may not be telling the truth or may be trying to hide something. Even lack of non-verbal clues can be an indication that a person is not telling the truth or trying to contrive /manipulate his actions to conceal his or her true feelings and thoughts.

Chapter One: Analyzing People Through Their Handwriting

Every person's handwriting is known to be as unique as their personality. You can make an in-depth analysis about everything from their behavior to personality to thought process. Graphology is the science of studying an individual's personality through how they write. Handwriting goes beyond putting a few characters on paper. It is about glimpsing into an individual's mind to decipher what they are thinking and how they are feeling based on their handwriting.

Here are some little-known secrets about speed reading a person through their handwriting.

Analyzing Individual Letters of the Alphabet

The manner in which a person writes his or her letters offers a huge bank of information about their personality, subconscious thoughts and behavioral characteristics. There are several ways of writing a single letter, and every person has their own distinct way of constructing it.

For example, putting a dot on the lower case "I" is an indication of an independent-spirited personality, originality and creative thinking. These folks are organized, meticulous and focused on details. If the dot is represented by an entire circle, there are pretty good chances of the person being more childlike and thinking outside the box. The manner in which a person constructs their upper case "I" reveals a lot about how they perceive themselves. Does their "I" feature the same size as the other letters or is it bigger/smaller compared to other letters?

A person who constructs a large "I" is often egoistic, self-centered, over confident and even slightly cocky. If the "I" is the size of other letters or even smaller than other letters, the person is more self-assured, positive and happy by disposition.

Similarly, how people write their lower case "t" offers important clues into their personality. If the "t" is crossed with a long line, it can be an indication of determination, energy, passion, zest and enthusiasm. On the other hand, a brief line across the "t" reveals lack of empathy, low interest, and determination. The person doesn't have very strong views about anything and is generally apathetic. If a person crosses their "t" really high, they possess an increased sense of self-worth and generally have ambitious objectives.

Similarly, people who cross their "t" low may suffer from low self-esteem, low confidence and lack of ambition. A person who narrows the loop in lower case "e" is likelier to be uncertain, suspicious and doubtful of people. There is an amount of skepticism involved that prevents them from being trustful of people. These people tend to have a guarded, stoic, withdrawn and reticent personality. A wider loop demonstrates a more inclusive and accepting personality. They are open to different experiences, ideas and perspectives.

Next, if an individual writes their "o" to form a wide circle, they are most likely people who very articulate, expressive, and won't hesitate to share secrets with everyone. Their life is like an open book. On the contrary, a closed "o" reveals that the person has a more private personality and is reticent by nature.

Cursive Letters

Cursive writing gives us clues about people that we may otherwise miss through regular writing. It may offer us more comprehensive and in-depth analysis of an individual's personality.

How does a person construct their lower case cursive "I?" If it has a narrow loop, the person is mostly feeling stressed, nervous and anxiety. Again, a wider loop can be a sign that the individual doesn't believe in going by the rule book. There is a tendency to rewrite the rules. They are laidback, low on ambition and easy going.

Again, consider the way a person writes cursive "y" to gain more information about their personality. The length and breadth of letter "y" can be extremely telling. A thinner and slimmer "y" can be an indication of a person who is more selective about their friend circle. On the other hand, a thicker "y" reveals a tendency to get along with different kinds of people. These are social beings who like surrounding themselves with plenty of friends.

A long "y" is an indication for travel, adventure, thrills and adventures. On the other hand, a brief cursive "y" reflects a need to seek comfort in the familiar. They are most comfortable in their homes and other known territories. A more rounded "s" is a signal of wanting to keep their near and dear ones happy. They'll always want their loved ones to be positive and cheerful.

They will seldom get into confrontations and strive to maintain a more balanced personality. A more tapering "s" indicates a hard-working, curious and hard-working personality. They are driven by ideas and concepts. Notice how cursive "s" broadens at the lower tip. This can be a strong indication of the person being dissatisfied with their job, interpersonal relationships or life in general. They may not pursue their heart true desires.

Letter Size

This is a primary observation that is used for analyzing a person through their handwriting. Big letters reveal that the person is outgoing, affable, gregarious and extrovert. They are more social by nature and operate with a mistaken sense of pride. There is a tendency to pretend to be something they aren't. On the contrary, tiny letters can indicate a timid, reticent, introvert and shy personality. It can indicate deep concentration and diligence. Midsized letters mean that an individual is flexible, adjusting, adaptable and self-assured.

Gap Between Text

People who leave a little gap in between letters and words demonstrate a fear of leading a solitary life. These people always like to be surrounded by other folks, and often fail to respect the privacy and personal space of other people. People who space out their words/letters are original thinkers and fiercely independent. For them, they place a high premium on freedom and independence. There is little tendency for being overwhelmed by other people's ideas, opinions and values.

Letter Shape

Look at the shape of an individual's letters while decoding their personality. If the writing is more rounded and in a looped manner, the person tends to be high on inventiveness and imagination! Pointed letters demonstrate that a person is more aggressive and intelligent. The person is analytical, rational and a profound thinker. Similarly, if the letters of an alphabet are woven together, the individual is methodical, systematic and orderly. They will rarely work or live in chaos.

Page Margins

If you thought it's only about writing, think again. Even the amount of space people leave near the edge of the margin determines their personality. Someone who leaves a big gap on the right side of the margin is known to be nervous and apprehensive about the future. People who write all over the page are known to have a mind full of ideas, concepts and thoughts. They are itching to do several things at once, and ae constantly buzzing with ideas.

Slant Writing

Some people show a marked tendency for writing with a clear right or left slant, while other people write impeccably straight letters. When a person's letters slant towards the right, he or she may be affable, easy going, good natured and generally positive. These people are flexible, open to change and always keen on building new social connections.

Similarly, people who write slanting letters that lean towards the left are mostly introverts who enjoy their time alone. They aren't very comfortable being in the spotlight and are happy to let others hog the limelight. A straight handwriting indicates rational, level headed and balanced thinking. The person is more even-tempered, grounded and ambivalent.

There is a tiny pointer here to avoid reading people accurately. For left-handed people, the analysis is the opposite. When left handed people have their letters slanting to the right, they are shy, introverted and reserved. However, if their letters slant to the left, they may be outgoing, gregarious and social extroverts.

Writing Pressure

The intensity with which an individual writes is also an indicator of their personality. If the handwriting is too intense and full of pressure (there is indentation), the individual may be fiery, aggressive, obstinate and volatile. They aren't very open to other people's ideas, beliefs and opinions. There is a tendency to be rigid about their views.

On the contrary, if a person writes with little pressure or intensity, they are likely to be empathetic, sensitive and considerate towards other people's needs. These people tend to be kind, enthusiastic, passionate, lively and intense.

Signature

A person's signature reveals plenty about an individual's personality. If it isn't comprehensible, it is a sign that he or she doesn't share too many details about themselves. They fiercely guard their private space and are reticent by nature. On the contrary, a more conspicuous and legible signature is an indication of a self-assured, flexible, transparent, assured, confident and satisfied personality. They are generally content with what they've accomplished and display a more positive outlook towards life.

Some people scrawl their signature quickly, which can be an indication of them being impatient, restless, perpetually in a hurry and desiring to do multiple things at one time. A carefully written and neatly organized signature is an indication of the person being diligent, well-organized and precision-oriented.

Signatures that finish in an upward stroke demonstrate a more confident, fun loving, ambitious and goal-oriented personality. These people thrive on challenges, aren't afraid of chasing these dreams. Similarly, signatures that finish with a downward stroke are an indication of a personality that is marked by low self-esteem, lack of self-confidence, low ambition and a more inhibited personality. These folks are likelier to be bogged down by challenges and may not be too goal oriented.

Stand Out Writing

If a particular piece of writing stands out from the other text, look at it carefully to understand an individual's personality.

For example, if the text is generally written in a more spread out and huge writing, with only some

123

parts of the text stuck together, the person may most likely to be an uncertain, dishonest or mistrustful individual, who is trying to conceal some important information.

Concluding

Though studying an individual's handwriting can offer you accurate insights about his or her personality, it isn't completely fool proof. There are several other factors that are to be taken into consideration to analyze a person accurately. It has its own shortcomings and flaws. At times, people may write in a hurried manner, which can impact their writing. Similarly, the way people construct their resume or application letter may dramatically vary from the manner in which they may write a to-do list or love letter.

If you want an accurate reading of someone's personality, consider different personality analysis methods like reading verbal and non-verbal communication techniques. Various techniques may offer you a highly in-depth, insightful, precise and comprehensive method of understanding a person's inherent personality.

Chapter Two: Tips For Uncovering Insights About Other People's Values

Mind reading isn't about drinking some magic potion and developing telepathic powers overnight. It is a science that is carefully nurtured and mastered by people to attain success in their daily life. Reading or analyzing people is a valuable skill that can come handy in any situation from approaching your manager for a raise to understanding a customer's needs to impressing a prospective date.

Here are some proven tips for deciphering people's values, wishes and desires through their thoughts, behavior and actions.

Watch For Hot Buttons

What are the emotional stimulants of a person you are studying? What is their comfort zone?

Identifying people's emotional triggers is a great way of gaining insight into their beliefs, value system and wishes.

A handy tip for learning more about a person's ideologies and values is to pose open ended questions to them. Rather than asking close-ended yes/no questions, pose queries that urge them to offer more in-depth responses. This can provide a glimpse into an individual's values.

Watch Out For Generational Differences

Though this is not a 100 percent fool proof method for analyzing a person's values, it can be an effective baseline for reading their personality through the manner in which they view the world. Generational differences may be more fascinating and insightful than people believe. While millennials focus on establishing more non-personal communication channels through social media or messenger.

On the other hand, bloomers may prefer face to face interactions where they can establish more meaningful and personal connections with others. They seek to set-up relationships where verbal and non-verbal signals are effective to make the most of their communication. Identifying an individual's generation can help to read them or try to establish a favorable rapport with them.

For example, if you want to close the deal with a youngish CEO you know there are lower chances of them wanting to complete the formalities face to face. They may be people who are comfortable with technology and sending emails back and forth. Their value system or way of working may be more determined by technology than by the old-fashioned route of taking potential clients and business associates on elaborate lunches and dinners. Knowing a person's generation can help you gain insights into another person's values, beliefs and principles.

Handling Power and Authority

The manner in which a person handles power reveals a lot about their values, beliefs and character. What is the individual's overall attitude towards people who they perceive to be lower in status? How do they treat servers, waiters and other people who can't do much for them or who we perceive to be beneath us in the status quo?

Listen to them talk to a customer service personnel. How do they air their grievances? What is the person's overall outlook towards animals and children? The way people treat other people who can't return their favors says a lot about their values. Are they generally rude to individuals who aren't as powerful as them? Do they indulge in more magnanimous or selfless acts? This reveals an individual's real colors.

Look at the Person's Contact List

It isn't a secret that a man is known for the company he keeps. One of the best ways for gaining insights into a person's value system and needs is through their friend circle. Are they with the same set of people since the last few years? Are they the leaders or followers within their social circle? Do they influence other people or are they influenced by the decisions and tastes of others? What are the types of people they dislike and like?

When you want to know more about someone's values, attitude, beliefs and principles, ask them about the type of people they avoid. This is a brilliant way to know their ideologies. They will always avoid people whose values clash with theirs. For example, when people I pose this question to tell me that they avoid people who are high-handed or deceitful, it is evident that they are more drawn towards honest and down to earth folks. Similarly, a person who says he/she don't like to mingle with people who are always partying may be more focused, goal-oriented and hard working. They are hard-working and want to achieve a lot in life.

If you notice carefully, you will identify a clear pattern in everyone they avoid. These traits reveal their own set of values. For example, sometimes you will notice that you just won't like certain people or you may subconscious avoid them. On closer scrutiny, you'll realize that they may all be ineffective listeners who do not show consideration for other people's thoughts, opinions, beliefs and feelings.

They may be more focused on being heard and putting their point across than listening to others. All this will help you realize that people who dislike or avoid such people may boast of a more empathetic personality that places a high premium on tuning in to other people's emotions.

Language

A person's beliefs, values, desires and principles are to a large extent revealed by their words. According to psychologists, we tend to emphasize on adjectives than pronouns while speaking, which offers subconscious indications of our persona. A high number of personal pronouns demonstrate an egocentric, selfish and self-centered personality. It can also be an indication of increased self-awareness, honesty, integrity.

There are other things that determine an individual's personality. For example, if a person is using big words or fancy terms to expresses their point of view, he or she may possess a desire to be constantly accepted or validates by others. There is a strong tendency to fit in or impress others. The individual may have faced rejection during their childhood, which led them to develop low self-confidence, low self-esteem and feeling of never being good enough.

On the other hand, people who use simpler words and phrases to express themselves are logical, self-assured and rational people who are confident in their abilities. They don't seek acceptance or validation from others and are fairly firm in their decision making. People who use words such as "but", "except" and "without" are mostly honest and truthful people who won't hesitate to share details.

Notice how people who are mostly happy, positive and content do not use "I" often. Similarly, usage of "he", "they" "she" etc. are more focused on others. They place the other person first in a relationship, while their own needs are put on the backburner. Even the kind of humor and jokes a person shares can tell a lot about their values, character, personality and attitude.

Don't we all love celebrities to engage in self-depreciating humor? Or for that matter anyone who cracks jokes about themselves! It is a sign of high confidence, self-assuredness and self-esteem.

These people are confident and secure enough to poke fun at themselves. They don't think or care much about the opinion other people hold of them, which makes them take potshots at themselves freely.

On the other hand, people who are quickly offended by jokes directed towards them may not have a very high self-esteem or may be suffering from an inferiority complex. A deep seated feeling of insecurity or an inferiority complex makes them easily offended by jokes directed towards them. Thus a person's approach to humor along with the language they use can offer plenty of insights into their value system.

Reaction to Criticism

The manner in which a person responds to criticism reveals plenty about their values. What is a person's reaction to facing criticism? Do they get defensive, angry and foul mouthed? Do they fly into a quick fit of rage? Do they accept their shortcomings with grace? People who handle criticism with graceful are more confident, self-assured, frank and forth coming! They aren't egoistic by nature and consciously work on their limitations.

On the contrary, people who don't take criticism too well may most likely be suffering from an inferiority complex, low self-esteem and inflated ego issues. They may need constant validation and appreciation. In their eyes, they can seldom be wrong. These folks may suffer from a high sense of self-entitlement or a misplaced sense of self-importance. They tend to be egoistic, self-centered and selfish by nature, which means you'll have to employ a lot of tact and diplomacy while dealing with these people.

How Does a Person Spend Their Money and Time?

Time and money are some of the most important resources of a person's life, and the manner in which he or she utilizes these precious resources says a lot about their values. Do people spend a lot of time and money on building a solid long-term future for themselves of their loved ones? Do they focus on acquisition of knowledge, learning, classes, skills and education?

Do they utilize their free time for upgrading their skills or waste it on frivolous pursuits? What are their pursuits, interests and hobbies? Don't scan people's expenses with a magnifying glass now. All you need to do is observe how people use their valuable

Gut Feeling

We can master all the people analyzing methods of the world and still rely on our gut feeling when it comes to reading people. If you have a specifically terrible feeling about someone and can't peg it to a logical thought, it may be an instinctive or gut feeling.

If you think your intuition or gut feeling isn't rooted in a scientific process, think again. What is termed a scientific process is closely connected to the limbic brain. It is a reaction to subconscious clues that the conscious mind has missed. If you develop a feeling that something or someone isn't right, your gut feeling may be bang on.

A Person's Reaction to No

How a person reacts to someone who refuses their request says a lot about them. Are they respectful and graceful in the face of rejection? Do they accept it graciously? Do they respond in a more violent, aggressive and volatile manner? Do they respect people's wishes and boundaries? Does the person manipulate people into turning their no into a yes? How a person reacts to refusals can speak volumes about their values and character.

Chapter Three: Reading People Through Their Immediate Environment

An individual's immediate environment can speak a lot about their personality, thought process, behavioral traits and values. Of course, this isn't a pop psychology quiz that pops on your social media timeline every now and then about your hairstyling preferences and nail paint colors determining your personality. These are solid, proven and scientific methods for making an educated guess about people through their immediate environment or the manner in which they live. There are clear psychological concepts and principles based on which you can tell a lot about a person through their environment. Here are some fabulous tips for analyzing a person through their surroundings.

The Closet

The mess within your physical environment is indicative of the chaos in the mind. This isn't about judging people through their environment; it is about analyzing people through their thought driven actions. It is reading a person through their thoughts, which eventually leads to the creation of the immediate environment.

A well-organized, efficient and systematic work station or desk is indicative of clear thoughts, clarity of decisions, good time management skills, and a need to get things done. The person is more goal driven and is driven by a desire to take up challenging tasks.

On the contrary, a messy, unclean and disorganized desk can be an indication of a chaotic mind that is filled with nervous and anxious thoughts. These people may suffer from low self-esteem, low self-confidence and other issues. It can also been observed that excessive cleanliness can be a sign of mental disorders like obsessive compulsive disorder and reveal a more nervous or anxious mind that is filled with uncertainties and a low self-esteem. There is an obsessive need to keep spaces clean and organized, which reveals a sense of inadequacy and disorderliness in the mind. The person may be trying to compensate for something they believe they lack by keeping their surroundings extra clean.

What is the first thing you think when you see a disorderly work or home space? Again, this isn't about being judgmental but reading or analyzing people through their immediate environment and setting. A cluttered space is often an indication of a cluttered mind. It can also mean that the person is a multi-tasker, who is keen on getting several things at a time. People who are busy or engaged in multiple activities seldom have the time or energy to organize their work space. As a result, it is left unattended or in a complete disarray. At times, a disorganized space can signal a plain lazy personality that reveals lack goals and clarity in life.

Again, you'd need to know more y digging a little deep rather than making sweeping judgments based on the space alone. It has been noticed that folks with a gregarious and social personality thrive in chaos around them. Peek into their drawers, and they are most likely kept in a disorganized and predictably messy manner. They aren't inward driven or believe in giving time to reflection, thoughts and organizing their space.

Introverts, on the other hand, are more reflective and contemplative y nature. Since they are inward directed, a lot of their time is spent in diligently organizing, arranging, managing and prioritizing their things. These things give them more clarity of thought and ideas upon reflection. Most people, however fastidious about cleanliness, have concealed spaces that are a complete mess.

These are generally areas that aren't frequently accessed. If these inaccessible areas are kept sparkling clean too, the person is most often suffering from a deep seated anxiety of nervousness disorder. These people are generally control freaks who are obsessed with the idea of controlling things around them to an unhealthy level.

Research also reveals that a disorganized, chaotic and unclean environment indicates creativity and innovativeness. People living or working in such messy and disorganized conditions tend to generate forward-thinking, resourceful and path-breaking solutions. Yes, the cliché about a scientist, writer or artist sporting a messier look and unkempt hair may actually be true from a personality-psychological angle.

Colors

What do colors within a person's immediate space reveal about him or her? The first thing that people probably look at when they enter someone's home or office is the color scheme used to do up the space. Bright, dazzling and bold colors instantly draw our attention to the space, while cool colors create a softer and more tranquil atmosphere. An individual's color choice can demonstrate a lot about their personality. For example, if the person has an inherent penchant or bold and vivid colors like red, purple, orange, magenta etc., they may be more adventurous, experimental and risk taking by nature. They aren't shy about expressing their thoughts and are constantly seeking new experiences. It signifies an outgoing, gregarious, unafraid and bold personality. These people aren't afraid to call a spade a spade.

On the other hand, people opting for cooler and more subtle shades may be reflective, quiet, restrained and analytical by nature. They are generally deep thinkers, who do not make hasty decisions. Their decisions are made after considering all possible options.

People who are inward focused will most likely have their homes done up in soft, subtle and solid hues, marked by muted patterns. Extroverts, on the other hand, tend to opt for more old, vibrant and experimental prints. Since they are more social and gregarious by nature, there is an inherent need to impress people. Extroverts are more outwardly focused, which means their decisions are more determined by what they think will please people around them.

Introverts seldom display this need to impress others and will often downplay themselves and their surroundings in a bid to avoid being noticed. Unlike extroverts, they are uncomfortable at the prospect of being the center of attention.

Prints and Designs

It may sound funny (or intriguing if you are like me). However, the prints or designs used to do up a person's home or office décor, or even their attire can be very telling about their personality. For example, bright, bold, large and vibrant prints can signify an uninhibited personality that is more self-assured, opinionated and seldom overwhelmed by other people's opinion. These people are fiercely original in their thoughts, opinions and actions. They often have their own opinion on multiple issues and are rarely influenced by the thoughts, opinions and ideas of other people.

Likewise, quirky prints such as graffiti, pop art, animal motifs and polka dots can reveal a penchant for fun and creativity. It is an indication of a creative, independent thinking and original personality. The person isn't afraid to express themselves and is least concerned about fitting in with the crowd. They yearn to stand out rather than fit in. These are your path-breakers, rebels and trend-setters.

Geometric prints can demonstrate an inclination towards order, symmetry and organization. People who wear a lot of geometric prints or have their homes/offices done up in predominantly geometric prints may reveal an affinity for balance, orderliness and analysis. There is a deep-seated need to have everything in order.

In an interesting study conducted by Yale researchers, it was revealed that people who spend hours taking showers or in the bath are generally lonely or emotionally deprived people who seek warmth from the bath to compensate for the emotional warmth in their lives. Makes sense, doesn't it?

Do you a wall filled with motivational quotes and inspiring messages in your home or office? You may want to read this then. Psychologists have researched that people having a wall filled with inspirational quotes and messages are more often than not possess neurotic tendencies. These people utilize their environment or the space around them for soothing their nerves and helping them navigate the storms in their life. Of course, don't automatically assume that something is not quite normal about a person when you spot a wall filled with motivational posters. The best way to gather more clues is to talk to the person. Observe verbal and non-verbal clues carefully to gain deeper insights into their personality.

Old Stuff

Ever noticed how some people's homes resemble a junkyard because they store all the old and unwanted stuff? There are old uniforms, sports jerseys they've long outgrown, clothes that don't fit them any longer and other memorabilia that has no place in their current lives. These are most likely folks who are unable to discard their past and move on. They are unable to let go of the past and move ahead. There is a need to cling on to the past and a refusal to look into the future. Hoarding objects may mean that they are still emotionally connected with memories attached to these belongings.

For example, if you are still holding on to a dress that you've long outgrown because it was gifted to you by a former lover, you are probably unwilling to come to terms with the fact that the relationship is over. You are still emotionally clinging on to the relationship instead of moving on and looking into the future. There is a tendency to be closely attached to people and memories that these objects represent at a subconscious level.

Chapter Four: Judging a Book by Its Cover

When you walk into a book store, how do you judge which book to pick up and which to pass? If you are like me, you are guilty of picking up books that have fancy titles, attractive covers and lots of visually arresting features. Accuse me of being shallow, but I also look at the quality of paper. Yes, judging a book by its cover is something we've all done at some point or the other.

We've all been fed on the belief that judging a book by its cover is not the right way to do it. However in a time and attention pressed world, where we rarely have the time to read people comprehensively, we seldom have an option but to analyze and speed people to make quick decisions about them. Reading a book by its cover or speed reading people may not be such a bad thing in today's times. People's outer appearances can often help you make solid and reliable conclusions about their personality. The subconscious visual that you form about an individual through their appearance is often accurate.

I know plenty of psychologists who believe that making snap judgments about people based on their appearances is an extremely narrow way of looking at it. However, the way a person treats himself or herself just as he/she treats his/her immediate environment can reveal a lot about their inherent personality. It can help you a gain a deeper understanding of their personality to make the communication even more meaningful.

The way a person dresses or maintains their outer appearance can reveal a lot about their internal feelings. Their exterior can often be a near accurate indicator of their thoughts, emotions and feelings. Ever noticed how when you are completely dejected or sad, you don't bother about how your hair or face looks? You don't have the inclination or zest to look good.

Similarly, when you are feeling more positive and upbeat, you will invest extra effort in looking good and feeling wonderful about yourself. People are well-dresses or sport a neatly-groomed appearance to gain respect or validation from others. They may want people to perceive them in a more positive light. It can also be a sign of high self-confidence, power and authority. People in positions of power and authority may also be wealthy, which gives them the resources to be expensively dressed and groomed. It can be a sign of influence, power and confidence. These folks are viewed in a more positive or flattering light by other people.

Here are some tips for reading people through their cover or outer appearance to make a near-accurate analysis of their personality or behavioral characteristics.

Good Influencers and Negotiators

Imagine a scenario where a plain looking person is selling you something you don't really need. He/she is plain looking and not very attractively dressed or groomed. Would you buy from him or her? The person doesn't appear like they are in a commanding or influential position when it comes to negotiations.

Now imagine another scenario where an extremely attractive, well-dressed and nattily groomed salesperson walks up to you and introduces themselves to you. Again, you don't really need what they are selling but you still listen to everything because the person is cute-looking, friendly and speaks with oodles of charm. By the end of their sales pitch, you realize that you can, in fact, use the product they are selling.

Attractive and well-groomed people have the power to influence people's decisions, however hollow it may seem. Of course, it isn't simply about wearing good clothes and looking good and ignoring everything else. There is a natural confidence and ease with which these people operate. Other factors such as friendliness, conversational skills, intelligence and other things matter too. This should explain why some people invest a bomb in maintaining their wardrobes and appearance.

Introverts and Extroverts

Extroverts thrive on adventure, new experiences, and risks. Their brains process dopamine starkly differently than it is processed in a person who is more inward driven or introverted. These thrill seekers think fast, act faster and are prone to be more impulsive when it comes to decision making. They will move and walk fast, which means they are at a greater risk of injuries.

This can be slightly stretched to conclude that people who have more injury scars or casts have higher chances of being extroverts. Their thrill seeking disposition and brain makes them more prone to accidents and injuries. Yes, these are the people who won't think twice before jumping out of a window to escape an adulterous confrontation.

Similarly, while introverts are more likely to observe your shoes and look at your feet while talking, extroverts will look you directly in the eyes while speaking. Since introverts are more inward driven and reflect upon their options before making a decision, they tend to seize/observe people. There is a tendency to look down at a person's feet because of the awkwardness involved in looking away from a person while speaking rather than looking into their eyes. To avoid this uncomfortable situation of looking everywhere around the eyes, introverts will glance at a person's shoes or feet while thinking.

Since extroverts are more outward driven and focused, they will look people in the eyes while talking. There is a tendency to experience rather than think, which means all their efforts are directed towards experiencing or listening to people instead of thinking about what people are talking. They'll seldom look in different directions (unless they are lying or there's another clear reason for the mismatch in behavior) and will have their eyes firmly fixated on the person they are speaking to.

Blue eyes and light, blonde hair has almost always been closely linked with extroversion. However, there isn't a conclusive study to support this view. More than anything, it is a popularly peddled media notion that is completely supported by the Hollywood and Disney brigade.

There is a definite bias towards light eyes and hair each time a character has to be represented as an extrovert. Ariel, Belle and Hercules are all Disney characters who've been portrayed as introverts with light hair and eyes. Today, you can't go about judging people's personality through the color of their eyes or hair because people are dying their hair and changing colored contact lenses faster than you can say personality.

Reading People Through Their Attire

Like we discussed earlier, the manner in which a person dresses reveals a lot about their personality. Neatly dressed and groomed people may have an inherent need to be respected and accepted within their social group. They may have a deep need to fit in or be validated by others. At times, dressing excessively well or paying too much attention to one's appearance can be a sign of narcissism of self-obsession. The person may also be suffering from a deeply rooted inferiority complex or low self-esteem that they are trying to compensate for by dressing well.

Sometimes, people who pay too much attention to their grooming and appearance may believe that they aren't good enough for anything and may use their looks to cover up for the perceived inadequacies in their life.

One of my friends could never match up to her older sibling when it came to intelligence, social skills and talent. While the parents lavishly praised her older sister for being an intelligent and talent student, she (the younger sibling) wasn't believed to be striking or extra ordinary in anything. Throughout her growing up years, she believed she wasn't good at anything and sought constant validation from people through her looks and clothes. She became obsessed with her appearance and spent huge sums of money on grooming, beauty products, beauty treatments and makeovers.

Thus, an excessive need to look good and dress well can also be a clue to an inferiority complex marked personality. Know more about a person before you make snap judgments about their outer appearance. However, appearance along with other non-verbal clues can offer you plenty of insights into an individual's subconscious thoughts, feelings and preferences.

Chapter Five: Speed Reading People Through Their Photographs

There's no escaping people's pictures in the age of a constantly buzzing social media feed. Like it or hate it, people are going to pictures of themselves. However, the good news from the perspective of a person analyzer is you can gather plenty of clues for speed reading people even before you meet them simply by learning to read their photographs.

Imagine gaining some clues about a prospective employee before they come down for a face or face interview or learning more about a client before negotiating an important deal with them. How about picking the right date by gathering insights about his or her personality through their social media images? Every image of a person holds a fascinating amount of information, meaning, and an indication of his or her emotional state. We only have to be perceptive enough to watch out for these clues. Sometimes, we are so overcome by the aesthetics of the image or the photography that we completely miss the emotions behind the image.

This chapter attempts to offer you some insights about how people's photographs can be used for interpreting their values, personality and behavioral traits. There are some obvious and some subtle pointers about decoding an individual's personality through their photos. You'll learn to find more meaning and context within the images rather than viewing them as random shots.

Don't Be in a Rush

Since photographs capture moments where time freezes, you need to study the image carefully to avoid any biases or inaccurate readings about something that may have happened in a microsecond. This may be contrary to the fast-speed, short span of attention, limited energy and the multi-tasking disposition we display. Hit the brain's pause button, do some deep breathing and get yourself into slow motion before you begin analyzing people through their images. You need to approach the art of analyzing people with both curiosity and compassion.

Don't leave out any details Look at the entire image. What is it that holds your attention when you first look at the picture? What are the conspicuous aspects of the image? Slowly move your attention and awareness to the other parts of the images. Look at it from different angles and perspectives.

Pull the image closer to your vision to detect elements that would otherwise go unnoticed. There are plenty of subtle details that your eye may miss if you don't view it closely. Turning the image upside down or sideways allows you to view it from an unusual perspective, which can change your entire view point about the image. You'll end up noticing things you wouldn't have otherwise noticed.

Subjective Reactions

What is it that strikes you the most about an image when you see it for the first time? What emotions, feelings, thoughts and sensations overcome your mind when you look at the image on an instinctive level? Think of a single descriptive word or phrase as a caption or title for the image that captures your spontaneous reaction to the image.

Do you think the picture represents pride, anger, anxiety, relief, frustration, confinement, exhaustion, success, elation, exhilaration, smoothness, rage, sadness and other compelling emotions? Your gut level reaction offers a clue on what you are thinking about the person.

While observing or analyzing people through their photographs, one of the most important considerations is your instant or an immediate reaction. However, you'll need to go beyond the first impression. You'll have to apply some amount of free association to analyze the person. Through free association, you are focusing on all elements of the image. Here are some questions you can ask yourself to facilitate greater free association to analyze people through images.

What does the picture remind you of?

What is the predominant emotion expressed by the person in the image?

What memories, incidents and experiences can you pull out from your own state of awareness on looking at the image?

How would you title the image?

However, when you are analyzing people through their pictures, beware against what psychologists terms projection. Projection is an unconscious process through which our own feelings, emotions, experiences and memories distort our perception of other people we are analyzing. You may invariably end up projecting your own feelings and experiences to them than trying to identify their personality. This is especially true for more ambiguous images. You don't know if you are rightly empathizing with people /reading them correctly or simply recalling your own experiences.

Sometimes, our own subjective reactions get in the way of reading people accurately. However, overcome this tricky situation and identifying when your own experiences and biases are getting in the way of analyzing people will help you be a more effective people analyzer.

Facial expressions

Human beings are innately expressive when it comes to tuning in to other people's facial expressions. What is your first reaction on looking at the person's face in the photograph? Psychologists have recognized seven basic emotions in a person – surprise, contempt, fear, sadness, anger, disgust and happiness. Keep these seven basic emotions in mind while analyzing people's expressions in images. At times, the expressions are underplayed or subtle, which makes it challenging to pin down the basic emotion.

Look for pictures where the person may not be aware that they are being clicked since that can be a more accurate representation of their subconscious mind.

Relationships

Again, you can tell a lot about the relationship between people by looking at their photographs. If a person is leaning in the direction of another person, there may be attraction or affection between the people. Similarly, if people are leaning in the opposite direction from each other, the relationship may lack warmth. If you notice a person clinging on to their partner's arm in almost every photograph, he or she may most likely be insecure about losing their partner. It may reveal a deep sense of insecurity or fear of losing their partner.

Try to predict the relationship between people through their body language in images. This can also be done in any public place where you have some time on hand to check people's body language, relationship equation and reactions. What are their feelings, emotions, thoughts and attitudes towards each other? Is there a pattern in the manner through which people touch, lean towards each other or look at one another? Does their body language reveal a lack of connectedness?

One of my favorite pastimes when it comes to analyzing people is looking at the photographs of celebrity couples and trying to read the nature of their relationship and/or their personality through their body language and expressions. I try to analyze if the image reveals intimacy, affection and positivity? Or it demonstrates tension, disharmony and conflict? Akeret, a well-known psychologist, believes that a photograph can also predict a relationships' future.

Some signs of comfort include smiling, holding hands, titling head in the direction of their partner. Hip to hip posture may indicate things are going great between the couple. How is the palmer touch? If it is touching with the full hand, the partners are close and affectionate. On the other hand, finger tips or fist touching can be a sign of being distant and reserved. Crossing legs may mean that they weren't very comfortable or open at the time the picture was taken. If you find a person crossing their arms or legs in almost every photograph, they may be suspicious, doubtful, cynical and unenthusiastic by nature.

Profile Pictures and Personality Traits

A big body of research suggests that human beings have the tendency to assess one another's personality through a quick glimpse. This is exactly why first impressions are so lasting. It takes us only 3-4 seconds to form an impression about a person through their verbal and non-verbal clues. Sometimes, they may not even say anything and we can subconsciously tune in to personality.

A recent research study reveals that you don't even have to meet a person once to form an opinion about him or her. All you need is a quick glance at their Facebook or even Tinder profile picture to gauge their personality. Here are the big five personality traits that are revealed through a person's profile picture.

The big five is pretty much the same as a scientific classification of personalities as Briggs-Myers is for recruitment. This personality approach classifies personalities on the basis of five fundamental traits, namely – introversion-extroversion, agreeableness, open to new experiences, conscientiousness and neuroticism.

A quick glance at your social media profile picture is sufficient for you to rate people correctly on the five fundamental dimensions. In a research conducted by PsyBlog, it was observed through a scientific analysis of the profile pictures of thousands of social media participant personalities that there were very specific and consistent patterns when it came to each of the five personality attributes.

For example, people scoring high on conscientiousness used images that were natural, filter-free, bright and vibrant. They were not afraid to express a large number of emotions through their pictures. If fact they displayed a higher number of emotions through their images than all other personality types.

You'll also find people scoring high on openness taking the most amazing shots. They are creative, innovative and resourceful. They'll play a lot with applications and filters owing to their creativity. Their pictures will be more artistic, unique and feature greater contrasts. Generally, people who score high on openness have their face occupy more space than any other feature in the photograph.

Extraversion folks will have perpetually broad smiles plastered on their faces. They will use collages and may surround their profile picture with used vibrant images. On the other hand, simple images with very little color or brightness is a strong indication of neuroticism. These pictures are likely to display a blank expression or in extreme cases may even conceal their face, according to the blog.

Agreeable people may often seem to the nicest people to get along with among all personality types. However turns out, they aren't really great photographers. Agreeable people are known to post unflattering images of themselves! However, even with the poor or unflattering images of themselves, they will be seen smiling or displaying a positive expression. The images will be vibrant, positive and lively.

Chapter Six: Spotting Deception Through Non-Verbal Clues

When people used to ask me during fun games what is what one superpower I would like to develop, I would always say the ability to spot liars and cheats. No, I didn't have any super detective or FBI aspirations! All I wanted to do was equip myself to be able to determine when people are lying and when they are telling the truth because this can save us plenty of heartbreak, relationship trouble, deals gone wrong and soured social relationships. If there's one superpower that can save you a lot of troubles and conflict, it is the ability to spot lies.

Though we can identify liars on an instinctive level, there are some clear verbal and non-verbal techniques that help you identify deception and lies.

Our unconscious or subconscious mind is capable of detecting liars fairly quickly and accurately. Fortunately, liars offer tons of signals through their words, voice and body language that can be quickly caught by an expert people analyzer. Here are some top tips for making you the ultimate lie detector.

1. Jerky Head Movements

People who aren't speaking the truth of trying to deceive others make sudden, unexpected and erratic head movements when they are confronted with a question. The head will retract slightly and move in a jerkier manner. In some cases, it may tilt a little. This happens in split seconds just before the person begins to reply to your question.

2. Direction of Eye Movements

When someone is lying, their eyes will generally move towards their right side. The eyes will go up, and then towards the right. This implies that the person is making up information. Since specific functions are performed by certain parts of our brain, the direction in which a person's eyes move can determine the function performed by their brain.

For example, when a person's eyes move to the upper left, we are most likely trying to recall information that is stored in the memory which means the person may be telling the truth. However, if a person's eyes move to the upper right, he or she isn't trying to recall or extract information from the memory. They are making up information or lying. When you confront someone with a question, their eye movements will reveal a lot about whether they are lying or speaking the truth. The reverse of this true for left –handed people.

In left-handed people, if the person looks to their upper right while thinking, they are trying to recall information from their memory. However, when they look at the upper left direction when confronted with a question, they are most likely making up facts or misleading you.

So before you term someone a liar, pleas ensure you know if the person is left or right handed.

Not just the direction of a person's eyes but also movements such as raising eyebrows or widening eyes is a non-verbal signal of deceit. People often look try to look stunned when their lies are called out. In a bid to appear surprised and shocked by your insinuation, they may widen their eyes or raise their eyebrows. It may be an act to make another feel guilty about accusing them.

3. The Projection Technique

Liars are brilliant at employing the projection technique. When confronted with a question, they will most likely come up with a counter question after pausing for a while. This is a typical response of liars. They will pause for a while to buy time and contemplate their response to being confronted.

This will be followed by an accusatory question directed towards you such as "Do you think I am a liar?" or "How can you accuse me of being a liar?" or "Why were you snooping around?" and similar other accusatory questions that are specifically designed to make you feel guilty about confronting them.

4. Nervousness

However smart deceivers think they are, they offer plenty of clues through their verbal and non-verbal communication. Watch out for their leg and feet movements because that is one of the most neglected parts of the body while we are interacting or communicating with people.

Liars can manipulate other signals such as maintaining eye contact or keeping a relaxed posture, since the fact that people who are speaking the truth always look you in the eye is now common and widely shared knowledge. They know that looking into a person's eyes while speaking can make them come across as more truthful.

However, some signals such as faking their leg or feet movements don't happen too effectively since these aren't very visible or noticeable areas of the body. This makes manipulating leg or feet movements near impossible. Plus it happens at such a subconscious level that it is near impossible to fake. When people lie or try to mislead others, their legs (or even feet) start twitching slightly. They may be fidgeting with their clothes or pretend to brush off lint from their shoulders.

Shrugging or slouching are other obvious signs of a liar.

5. Watch Out For Verbal Signals

While non-verbal signals can reveal a lot about whether a person is lying or telling the truth, his or her words can also be extremely revealing. People who are lying generally speak using a slower and more spaced out way. There are plenty of pauses that they use for buying time.

Their speech will most likely have a more uneven or inconsistent pitch. Liars will be more hesitant in the way they speak. Genuine people answer quickly, while false responses come up only after careful consideration of all options. The person will take more time to deliberate, which will slow their speech. It takes time to think of appropriate words when you are lying.

Also, people who lie or mislead others have the tendency to detach themselves from the situation. They will deny any responsibility or detach from the occurrence, which simply means they'll use lesser sentences in the active voice.

They will seldom use sentences that begin with "I" and will often use passive voice or speak in a manner that something happened to them rather than they did something. Liars will either offer very little details or a lot of details in a bid to cover the fact that they are lying. There is a tendency will volunteer with plenty of unnecessary details. They'll attempt to throw your questioning in another direction by offering a lot of details, most of which may be irrelevant, just to demonstrate that they are speaking the truth. They hope people will buy their 'innocence' if they give long and elaborate answers.

This makes liars use plenty of fluff words and filler and very little concrete details. They won't offer solid information. Their sentences will be long and yet not offer anything substantial. People who are lying with almost always never offer tiny and verifiable details. They will focus more on emotions or how hurt they are or how someone is feeling. The conversation or interaction will be more fraught with an apparent show of emotions rather than verifiable facts. Always confront a liar by asking them specifics, which only someone who us speaking the truth would know.

Even when you spot a clear contradiction in what they are saying and what you know is the truth, let them continue speaking. Give the confidence that you trust their version of what happened and allow them to give you even more clues of their lie. This can be used for confronting them at a later date. Let them go on and on with stories and created versions that will eventually help nail them. The idea is to catch them in their own spun web!

Liars will almost always detach themselves from an occurrence or event and focus on the other person or people. They will rarely use "I" or "me" while constructing their sentences since they are attempting to detach themselves from their falsehood at a subconscious level. They are not recollecting facts from their mind. Rather they are fabricating lies, which is why they are trying to distance themselves from their version of events. It happens at a very subtle and subconscious level, and they are obviously not aware of it (until they read this book that is!). There is a very strong need to psychologically distance or detach themselves from the situation

6. Physiological Effects

Lying produces plenty of psychological effects within the human body (which is what is captured by lie detecting machines) such as immediate blood vessels swelling, rapid heart rate, increases palpitations, sweating, itchy reaction on the skin and much more. When out blood vessels expand or experience swelling, the skin invariably begins to feel scratchy. This is why liars start feeling uncontrollably itchy when they lie. The itchy nose may not be such a myth after all and may have a deep physiological significance when it comes to spotting liars.

7. The Face Touch

The way in which a person touches their face demonstrates whether he or she is lying or speaking the truth. People who are lying will more often than not cover their mouth using their hands. This is a subconscious gesture to prevent spilling out information that they shouldn't or a way for them to suppress the urge of blurting out the truth. When people cover the mouth with their hands, the thumb will most likely be near the cheeks. Some fingers will be spread over the mouth to psychologically cover up.

Another sign of deception is when liars are confronted with the truth or a question and instead of answering the question; they break into a fake cough bout. This is nothing more than an attempt to buy time for making up tales.

8. How Are the Hands Positioned?

Keeping their hands at the back can be a sign of trying to conceal something. Liars will seldom reveal their palms or make an open palm gesture. People who are transparent, genuine and speaking the truth will keep their palms wide open, while those who are being deceitful or lying will turn their palms upside down.

It is a subconscious gesture that they have something to hide. Liars will often place their palms in their pocket to avoid revealing them to the other person, which is a near accurate indication of them wanting to conceal facts.

9. The Voice Raise

When a person's voice rises slightly or starts becoming shakier owing to muscle contraction, the person may be undergoing some form of stress. Their voice inflection may be higher than normal, and there may be palpable tension within the voice. An expert people reader will not miss these clues.

10. Variance in Confidence

Carefully observe the variation in a person's confidence when they are confronted with a question or the truth. They may either freeze or become extremely verbose, thus revealing lack of confidence or control. If you want to get the person to giveaway more clues about their lies and deceit, employ a technique used by investigators. Rather than making the communication appear like an interrogation, make it more conversational.

Liars more often than not give themselves away completely by being more illogical, sporadic and erratic in their responses. If you interact with them in a more conversation manner by letting their guard down, they will invariably give themselves away.

11. Look At A Person's Shoulders

Sometimes, a person's shoulders diminish or close in while lying. This is the exact opposite of an expanding posture, which indicates power, authority and self-confidence. By closing in their shoulders, the person is trying to diminish their posture because subconsciously and consciously too they are aware that they did something shameful, which reduces them in stature.

When they know they have done something wrong, the person's confidence invariably reduces. They are almost ashamed of their act, which leads them to form a more diminutive or reduced posture. Liars often conduct themselves with greater vulnerability. There is always a fear and insecurity that their lies will be caught, which leads them to hunching posture. When the elbows draw closer together, the individual takes on a posture that makes them look more diminutive in size, which is a sign of low confidence or vulnerability.

12. Microexpressions

Microexpressions occur in split seconds, which make them tough to fake. It is near impossible to work on or manipulate one's microexpressions even if people can mislead with their regular facial expressions. These happen so fast that there's no way a person can modify them unless he or she is a practiced manipulator who is aware of body language manipulation techniques. Laypeople, however, will seldom be able to fake microexpressions.

When a person isn't speaking the truth, their mouth will become slightly skewed. The eyes will subtly roll right after the person has spoken a lie. This is a near accurate microexpression of spotting deception. Other not so obvious microexpressions are a change in the color of an individual's cheeks, expanded nostrils, increased sweating, lip biting, and quick eye movements in all directions. These are nothing but signals of brain activity when a liar is processing information that isn't true. There are certain reactions in the brain based on the activity that is happening within it. These processes or reactions are closely connected with movements on the face or physiological facial reactions, which leads to microexpressions.

13. Pose Non-Threatening Questions

One of the best ways for identifying if a person is telling the truth is by posing more neutral and seemingly non-threatening questions. The idea is to get people to shed their guard and open up when you begin asking them questions.

Begin by establishing a baseline for the person's behavior. How does he or she normally behave? What is his or her predominant personality type? Then compare and contrast their current behavior with how they normally behave. Do you spot a clear mismatch? Start by engaging in small talk about the weather, hobbies, passions, weekend plans and other similar topics. Get them in a more relaxed, unguarded and normal state of mind! This will allow them to drop their guard and answer in a more relaxed manner.

Now closely observe their movements, expressions, eye movements, gestures, feet, posture and other non-verbal clues while they are speaking. Is the person looking directly into your eyes while speaking? Are they constantly shifting their gaze? Pose sufficient queries to establish a pattern.

My favorite technique when it comes to establishing a baseline behavior is asking them questions they are comfortable with and observe their body language. Note as much information as you can about their body language for this will give you a fairly good idea about their baseline or normal body language when they are comfortable discussing the topic at hand. Then gently shift to a topic that makes them uncomfortable or confront them with questions related to their lies.

Note any variance in the body language. Is there a clear mismatch in their body language from what it was when they were comfortable talking about a subject? Do they suddenly display feelings or discomfort or vulnerability? If there is a mismatch when you become more confrontational, they may have something to hide. If their body language suddenly changes when they are confronted, you may have to put pieces of the picture together to call out their lies.

Chapter Seven: The Attraction Body Language

You may be insanely attracted to a person but may not have the courage to ask them out owing to the prospect of facing humiliation and rejection. Imagine how easier things would be if you knew if they are as much into you as you are into them. Think of a situation where you've been set up on a blind date by enthusiastic friends or you find a date online, and really want to know if they are attracted to you. You may go out on a first date and come back not knowing whether the person really liked you or not!

Wouldn't it be nice if there could be a telepathic way to gauge if a person feels truly attracted towards you? How can you figure out if a person is genuinely attracted to you or is being plain nice to you because they don't want to hurt you (yes, we've all been guilty of this)?

Can verbal and non-verbal clues help you establish a potential lover's true feelings, emotions, thoughts and intentions? Can body language be used for unlocking a person's subconscious mind to tune in to their innermost feelings and thoughts about you? Use these secret attraction clues (that I rarely share with anyone) to help you gain increases social proof and experience more gratifying and fulfilling relationships.

The Attraction Signals

When an individual is attracted to you, they will transmit plenty of feel good or positive non-verbal clues for you to tune in to at a subconscious level. To begin with, when a person is deeply attracted to you, their body will almost always face you.

Everything from their face to their chest, shoulders and feet will most likely be pointed in your direction. The person will lean closer while speaking or interacting with you in a bid to get closer on a subconscious and emotional level. When they stand at a distance of under four feet away from you, they are keen on entering or personal space or inner circle of friends. They are trying to physically enter your inner zone or personal space to make a place for themselves in it.

If you want to know if a person is keenly into you or interested in you, don't give in to their interest straightaway. Rather than facing them, maintain a shoulder to shoulder position. If they person is truly interested in you, he or she will make an effort to win your attraction. Let them know that they've to win your attraction for you to stand facing them or mirror their attraction signals.

Leaning in the direction of a person is almost always a sign of attraction. We subconsciously lean towards people we are attracted to. When a person leans towards you in a group, it is clear that they are interested in you (or what you are speaking). Of course, sometimes a person may be simply keen on listening to what you are saying, in which case you will have to look at other clues. However, leaning towards a person within a group setting is a subconscious indication that they are drawn towards you.

Another sign of attraction includes seizing a person from up to down, and then down to up. This is a primitive way (which is still alive) for checking out the sexual potential of a prospective mate.

Together with other clues, uncrossed arms and legs can be a sign of attraction. Similarly, a broad smile dilated pupils and open palms can also reveal attraction. Head tilting is another sign of interest and engagement. It signals a person's desire to communicate to you that they are always around for you. Looking at a person in the eye for long while speaking can also be a huge sign of attraction. If you are attracted to a person or want to win their affection, avoid looking over their head or even all over the place. It reveals lack of interest and sensitivity, which will not give them the right signal.

Touch

Touch is a clue that an individual is completely comfortable in your presence. They may also be keen or getting to know more about you. They may get flirtatious or hit on you by playfully touching you. Some of the most common initial attractions signals are placing their hand over your hand, brushing their shoulder or leg against your shoulder or leg while talking to you and pretending to touch you accidently.

If you are confused about how to read a person's touches, observe how they touch another person versus how they touch you. If they are generally touchy-feely with everyone around, it is their baseline personality. However, if they make special exceptions in the manner in which they you, it is more often than not a sign of attraction. If the individual touches more than normal or in a different way, he or she may be attracted to you.

If you are attracted to a person, use body language to your advantage by conveying your feelings through non-verbal signals. Don't distance yourself from the person even if you don't want to send out very obvious signs of attraction. On a subconscious level, they may not realize they are attracted to you. Similarly, don't go all out and make the person step back in discomfort. Maintain a balance. Start with a light or playful tap on the shoulder or elbows. It is harmless yet reveals that a person likes you. Then gradually, move to touching their arm, wrist or back while talking. Make the touch more gradual and subtle so they don't wince or retreat with discomfort.

Mirroring

Mirroring happens at a deeply subconscious level and is one of the most reliable signals of a person's attraction. Watch out for people mirroring your actions. There is either a deeply seated need to be accepted or they are truly attracted to you. Sometimes after you've just met or been introduced to a person at a party, you'll notice that he or she starts mirroring everything from your words to your nods to your hand gestures to expressions.

People who don't know much about reading or analyzing people will often miss these clues. However, on a subconscious level, this is a sign that the person is seeking your acceptance or approval. When you are leaning against the bar, you'll notice a person come up to you and lean in the same position as you before striking up a conversation. They are doing nothing but attempting to mirror your actions in a bid to make you feel that they are one among your kind. People will hold their glass exactly in the manner in which you are holding yours or they may take a sip on their drink right after you do to show you that they are like you. The feeling of affiliating with people

on a psychological level drives people to mirror
their actions.

Conclusion

I sincerely hope it has offered you tons of proven strategies, tried and tested techniques and effective tips for reading people in multiple situations and life circumstances, while making you a perceptive people reader!

Whether you're trying to gauge what a potential client is thinking during a deal or if your hot new crush is attracted to you or if you want to hire perfect person for a role in your organization, this book presents a treasure casket of practical tips and wisdom nuggets to help you read people like books in varied situations. This, even with people who don't talk much because there are plenty of non-verbal clues!

The next step is to simply use this invaluable people reading handbook by implementing the strategies explained here in your everyday life. You aren't going to be an expert people reader overnight. It comes with lots of observation, consistency and practice.

Get into the habit of speed reading people using these strategies in several places from airports to bars to corporate boardrooms to cafes, when you have some free time at hand.

Finally, if you enjoyed reading the book, please take the time to share your thoughts by posting a review on Amazon. It'd be greatly appreciated.

Here's to being an awesome people reader, who can use the super power of analyzing people's thoughts, emotions and feelings to enjoy more rewarding and gratifying relationships.